"Graceful simplicity . . . Alvarez writes poems as impressive as her fiction."   —*Library Journal*

"Written with a novelist's sense of narrative and place, these poems forge ahead in language as plain and palpable as thick Caribbean light . . . laced with wisdom and humor. . . . Alvarez maps out the heart's ongoing journey . . . and the thin, precarious bridges we build from country to country, from silence to silence, from childhood to whatever place we invent for ourselves in the world."
     —*Miami Herald*

"Tracing a lyrical journey through the landscape of immigrant life, these direct, reflective, and often sensuous poems . . . take us across borders so slowly that only on reaching the other side can we see the distances we've come. . . . meticulous . . . assured. . . . Alvarez claims her authority as a poet with this collection."   —*Publishers Weekly*

"Playful and profound."
     —*San Francisco Chronicle Book Review*

"Complex . . . sensuous."   —*Arizona Republic*

JULIA ALVAREZ is the author of another book of poetry, *Homecoming,* and the novels *How the García Girls Lost Their Accents* and *In the Time of the Butterflies* (all available in Plume editions) and the forthcoming *¡Yo!* She is currently professor of English at Middlebury College in Vermont.

Julia Alvarez

THE OTHER SIDE
EL OTRO LADO

A PLUME BOOK

PLUME
Published by the Penguin Group
Penguin Books USA Inc., 375 Hudson Street, New York, New York 10014, U.S.A.
Penguin Books Ltd, 27 Wrights Lane, London W8 5TZ, England
Penguin Books Australia Ltd, Ringwood, Victoria, Australia
Penguin Books Canada Ltd, 10 Alcorn Avenue, Toronto, Ontario, Canada M4V 3B2
Penguin Books (N.Z.) Ltd, 182–190 Wairau Road, Auckland 10, New Zealand

Penguin Books Ltd, Registered Offices: Harmondsworth, Middlesex, England

Published by Plume, an imprint of Dutton Signet,
a division of Penguin Books USA Inc.
Previously published in a Dutton edition.

First Plume Printing, December, 1996
10 9 8 7 6 5 4 3

 REGISTERED TRADEMARK—MARCA REGISTRADA

The Library of Congress has catalogued the Dutton edition as follows:
Alvarez, Julia.
    The other side = El otro lado / Julia Alvarez.
        p.   cm.
    ISBN 0-525-93922-9 (hc.)
           0-452-27341-2 (pbk.)
    1. Dominican Americans—Journeys—Dominican Republic—
Poetry.   2. Hispanic American women—Poetry.   I. Title.
II. Title: Otro lado.
PS3551.L845O84   1995
811'.54—dc20   94-43847
                          CIP

Printed in the United States of America
Original hardcover design by Steven N. Stathakis

Bill

—a quien buscaba

Acknowledgments

I wish to thank the editors of the following magazines and anthologies in which these poems first appeared.

The Caribbean Writer: "Estel"
Chelsea: "Anatomy"
The George Washington Review: "Bilingual Sestina" and "Exile"
The Green Mountain Review: "Beginning Love" and "Bookmaking"
The Kenyon Review: "Mami and Gauguin"
Patchwork of Dreams: Voices from the Heart of the New America: The Spirit That Moves Us: "Queens, 1963"

Many thanks to Altos de Chavón for a residency that allowed me the time and place to work in the Dominican Republic, both on these poems as well as on projects in the village of Boca de Chavón. Thanks, too, to the National Endowment for the Arts for its support.

My deepest *gracias* to Judith Yarnall, who gave me extra ears, eyes, courage, and encouragement at different stages in the writing of these poems.

Special thanks to other helpful readers: Susan Bergholz, Rosemary Ahern, Barry Moser, Bob Pack, and Bill Eichner. And to Judith Liskin-

Gasparro, for teaching me the rules to my first tongue.

Para mis amigos, los chavoneros, con agradecimiento y profunda comprensión.

¡Virgencita, acompaña mi librito!

Contents

THE OTHER SIDE
EL OTRO LADO

I

Bilingual Sestina

Some things I have to say aren't getting said
in this snowy, blond, blue-eyed, gum-chewing English:
dawn's early light sifting through *persianas* closed
the night before by dark-skinned girls whose words
evoke *cama, aposento, sueños* in *nombres*
from that first world I can't translate from Spanish.

Gladys, Rosario, Altagracia—the sounds of Spanish
wash over me like warm island waters as I say
your soothing names: a child again learning the *nombres*
of things you point to in the world before English
turned *sol, tierra, cielo, luna* to vocabulary words—
sun, earth, sky, moon. Language closed

like the touch-sensitive *morivivi* whose leaves closed
when we kids poked them, astonished. Even Spanish
failed us back then when we saw how frail a word is
when faced with the thing it names. How saying
its name won't always summon up in Spanish or English
the full blown genie from the bottled *nombre*.

Gladys, I summon you back by saying your *nombre*.
Open up again the house of slatted windows closed
since childhood, where *palabras* left behind for English
stand dusty and awkward in neglected Spanish.
Rosario, muse of *el patio*, sing in me and through me say
that world again, begin first with those first words

you put in my mouth as you pointed to the world—
not Adam, not God, but a country girl numbering
the stars, the blades of grass, warming the sun by saying,
¡Qué calor! as you opened up the morning closed
inside the night until you sang in Spanish,
Estas son las mañanitas, and listening in bed, no English

yet in my head to confuse me with translations, no English
doubling the world with synonyms, no dizzying array of words
—the world was simple and intact in Spanish—
luna, sol, casa, luz, flor, as if the *nombres*
were the outer skin of things, as if words were so close
one left a mist of breath on things by saying

their names, an intimacy I now yearn for in English—
words so close to what I mean that I almost hear my Spanish
heart beating, beating inside what I say *en inglés*.

4

II

The Gladys Poems

Audition

Porfirio drove Mami and me
to Cook's mountain village
to find a new pantry maid.
Cook had given Mami a tip
that her hometown was girl-heavy,
the men lured away to the cities.
We drove to the interior,
climbing a steep, serpentine,
say-your-last-prayers road.
I leaned toward my mother
as if my weight could throw
the car's balance away
from the sheer drop below.
Late morning we entered
a dusty village of huts.

Mami rolled down her window
and queried an old woman,
Did she know of any girls
looking for work as maids?
Soon we were surrounded
by a dozen señoritas.
Under the thatched cantina
Mami conducted interviews—
a mix of personal questions
and Sphinx-like intelligence tests.
Do you have children, a novio?
Would you hit a child who hit you?
If I give you a quarter to buy
guineos at two for a nickel,
how many will you bring back?
As she interviewed I sat by,
looking the girls over;
one of them would soon
be telling me what to do,
reporting my misbehaviors.
Most seemed nice enough,
befriending me with smiles,
exclamations on my good hair,
my being such a darling.
Those were the ones I favored.
I'd fool them with sweet looks,
improve my bad reputation.
As we interviewed we heard
by the creek that flowed nearby
a high, clear voice singing
a plaintive lullaby . . .
as if the sunlight filling
the cups of the allamandas,

the turquoise sky dappled
with angelfeather clouds,
the creek trickling down
the emerald green of the mountain
had found a voice in her voice.
We listened. Mami's hard-line,
employer-to-be face
softened with quiet sweetness.
The voice came closer, louder—
a slender girl with a basket
of wrung rags on her head
passed by the cantina,
oblivious to our presence.
Who is she? my mother asked.
Gladys, the girls replied.
Gladys! my mother called
as she would for months to come.
Gladys, come clear the plates!
Gladys, answer the door!
Gladys! The young girl turned—
Abruptly, her singing stopped.

Gladys Singing

Gladys sang as she worked
in her high, clear voice,
mangulinas, merengues,
salves, boleros, himnos.
Why do you sing? I asked her
as she polished off a song
with a twirl of her feather duster.
Singing, she told me, *makes*
everything else possible.
She taught me *La cucaracha,*
Yo soy el aventurero,
Compadre Pedro Juan,
Guantanamera.
She swept and mopped, whistling
the lament of the sad *hidalgo;*

her hand as she washed windows
conducted a hidden combo;
she polished the mute mahogany
of the sideboard, humming quietly,
then belting out a song
when we heard the front door close,
Mami calling goodbye,
the car turning on the road.
Canta y no llores,
porque cantando se alegran,
Cielito Lindo, los corazones.
Together we polished the slats
of the sliding *salomónicas*
until they glowed the rich
rhythm of a *guaracha*;
we sang passionate *canciones,*
anthems or carols in season;
putting aside our brooms,
we danced energetic *merengues.*
I trained my tentative alto
to her silver bell soprano,
until we heard the car
roaring up the driveway,
the click of my mother's heels
metronomic at the entrance,
and we fell silent, knowing the rules,
as the door opened upon
rooms sparkling like jewels
in a mummy's lonely tomb.

Mami and Gauguin

Gauguin's barebreasted girls
hung above the sideboard
of our Dominican dining room.
When she judged I'd caught on
to table manners and could eat
everything on my plate,
Mami let me sit
at the tableclothed table
with an arsenal of silverware
in the high-ceilinged room,
two cushions on my chair
so that I was eye level
with the berry-red titties
of the Tahitian girls.
Their rich coffee-color skin

gleamed in the somber light
of the angled jalousie windows.
Their eyes watched my every move
as I twisted this way and that
trying to master the art
of making vegetables disappear
inside the centerpiece orchids.
Not with your hands!
Keep your mouth closed!
Did you chew that enough?
It was hard to enjoy
even old favorites
under the pomp and circumstances.
Ay, but the naked girls
with their ironic, narrowed eyes
in their splashes-of-color world
kept desire in my perspective.
Midmeal when there were guests
the annoying interrogation
began before dessert
could sweeten the silly question:
What do you want to be
when you grow up? —As if
girls had much of a choice—
a nun, a wife, a *jamona*
freeloading off the family.
Gladys, the maid, rolled by
with the trolley of silver platters,
glancing every now and then
at the scandalous bare breasts
of the young women her color
whose picture the *doña* hung
where the Virgencita belonged.

Mami was teaching her ways
so she could marry up—
maybe a chauffeur or *guardia*
A lady bends at the knees.
Button the last button.
But the naked native girls
with bold eyes and saucy mouths
belied Mami's bite-size,
high-collar, long-sleeve,
pureed-vegetables way
of being alive in the world.
Once I dared to contradict
pointing at my muses'
hibiscus-red lips and nipples.
That's art, Mami nodded,
smiling, her face soft
as the supple arms of the girls,
In art you can do what you want.
Dessert fork in hand, I practiced
on the gleaming white of my plate
signing my name with the flourish
of an artist on her canvas.

Grace

A soft rap at the door.
Gladys done with cleaning
visits me grounded
the long summery day
in my toy-stripped bedroom.
Through the angled jalousies
the afternoon sun streams in
imprisoning the floor
in a hundred little bars.
I hold out my arm,
sliding it up and down
as if an invisible shuttle
were weaving my young flesh.
I am learning I have a body.
I am responsible for its evil.

I lie in bed listening
to the happy shouts from the yard,
sisters and cousins playing
their games of innocent fun.
Then Gladys comes for a break,
sits on the edge of my bed,
her brown skin glistening
with hard-working sweat,
wet patches under her arms.
Because we fell from grace
this happens, the priest says,
sweat of our brow, sin,
sorrow, punishment, death.
Just beginning to accept
this legacy, I suspect
I'll keep falling into temptation.
Gladys eyes the empty shelf
where only schoolbooks remain
and trinkets not quite toys.
May I? she asks, taking down
the paperweight glass dome.
Inside, a tiny deer
grazes alone in a wood
of miniscule Christmas trees.
She gives the ball a shake.
A hundred dust motes flutter
to the cold, cold ground.
The deer nuzzles in search
of something he cannot find.
Then as if all the grains
in an hourglass had dropped
the future into the past,
the snow settles on the trees,

the painted back of the deer,
the chandelier of his antlers,
the bare ground . . .
                              How still
we see the world lie.
Before anyone comes in
footprinting the virgin white,
or cries from the yard recall
the empty hours ahead,
or from the kitchen Cook calls
for Gladys to clean the rice,
we sit released, peering
at this tiny, becalmed Eden
as at the End when our sins,
the priest says, will be forgiven.
Then Gladys eyes me, smiling.
I pick up the snowy scene,
give it a punishing shake,
and the storm again begins.

Proof

Papi brought home a puppy
stained with ink spots, a gift
from a grateful American
whose tonsils he'd taken out.
Alone with the speckled puppy
I tried rubbing off the spots
until Looky yelped in pain.
The maids wouldn't come close
fearing the devil's work.
Only Gladys like doubting Thomas
touched the dots wanting proof
the dog wasn't just another
made-in-the-USA gadget.
I, too, doubted he was real.
Until in a book Tía brought

from a trip to Nueva York,
I saw towers touching the sky,
a giant Virgin with tiny people
walking inside her halo.
I showed the pictures to Gladys
who wet her finger to turn
the pages as I had taught her.
Her hand flew up to her forehead
tracing a sign of the cross.
Let's make each other a promise—
I nodded, eager for pacts,
especially those confirmed
with blood or dare-you swigs
from coca-colas kept for company.
Swear that whoever goes first
to the USA land of marvels
will come back and report
if all of these are just stories.
Outside from his new pen
Looky barked as living proof
the extraordinary was alive
right under our very noses.

Abandoned

Gladys, where did you go?
You disappeared one Sunday
while we were away at church
with your paperbag of clothes
supposedly by your choice.
In hushed whispers I heard
that your fingers had been picking
our absent-minded pockets.
Another version ran
that an uncle's eye had been caught
roving by a jealous aunt.
Forlorn at your disappearance
I walked the immaculate house
now silent of your singing,
knocking cushions on the floor,

smudging the polished glass
on the doors of the china cabinet.
At the linen closet I toppled
a neat stack of kitten-soft towels,
breathing in the clean smell
of sheets you'd hung out to dry
singing the whole while.
All the napkins you had folded
in squares with monograms showing
I heaped onto the floor!
My socks I unballed in the drawer,
unlined my shoes in the closet.
You had left the world in order,
your swan song a clean house.
Quietly, working havoc
—spilling, staining, spoiling—
I tried to mar this perfection,
to recall you to your creation.

III

Making Up the Past

Exile

Ciudad Trujillo, New York City, 1960

The night we fled the country, Papi,
you told me we were going to the beach,
hurried me to get dressed along with the others,
while posted at a window, you looked out

at a curfew-darkened Ciudad Trujillo,
speaking in worried whispers to your brothers,
which car to take, who'd be willing to drive it,
what explanation to give should we be discovered . . .

On the way to the beach, you added, eyeing me.
The uncles fell in, chuckling phony chuckles,
What a good time she'll have learning to swim!
Back in my sisters' room Mami was packing

a hurried bag, allowing one toy apiece,
her red eyes belying her explanation:
a week at the beach so Papi can get some rest.
She dressed us in our best dresses, party shoes.

Something was off, I knew, but I was young
and didn't think adult things could go wrong.
So as we quietly filed out of the house
we wouldn't see again for another decade,

I let myself lie back in the deep waters,
my arms out like Jesus' on His cross,
and instead of sinking down as I'd always done,
magically, that night, I could stay up,

floating out, past the driveway, past the gates,
in the black Ford, Papi grim at the wheel,
winding through back roads, stroke by difficult stroke,
out on the highway, heading toward the coast.

Past the checkpoint, we raced towards the airport,
my sisters crying when we turned before
the family beach house, Mami consoling,
there was a better surprise in store for us!

She couldn't tell, though, until . . . until we were there.
But I had already swum ahead and guessed
some loss much larger than I understood,
more danger than the deep end of the pool.

At the dark, deserted airport we waited.
All night in a fitful sleep, I swam.
At dawn the plane arrived, and as we boarded,
Papi, you turned, your eyes scanned the horizon

as if you were trying to sight a distant swimmer,
your hand frantically waving her back in,
for you knew as we stepped inside the cabin
that a part of both of us had been set adrift.

Weeks later, wandering our new city, hand in hand,
you tried to explain the wonders: escalators
as moving belts; elevators: pulleys and ropes;
blond hair and blue eyes: a genetic code.

We stopped before a summery display window
at Macy's, *The World's Largest Department Store*,
to admire a family outfitted for the beach:
the handsome father, slim and sure of himself,

so unlike you, Papi, with your thick mustache,
your three-piece suit, your fedora hat, your accent.
And by his side a girl who looked like Heidi
in my storybook waded in colored plastic.

We stood awhile, marveling at America,
both of us trying hard to feel luckier
than we felt, both of us pointing out
the beach pails, the shovels, the sandcastles

no wave would ever topple, the red and blue boats.
And when we backed away, we saw our reflections
superimposed, big-eyed, dressed too formally
with all due respect as visitors to this country.

Or like, Papi, two swimmers looking down
at the quiet surface of our island waters,
seeing their faces right before plunging in,
eager, afraid, not yet sure of the outcome.

Papi Working

The long day spent listening
to homesick hearts,
the tick tock of the clock—
the way Americans mark time,
long hours, long days.
Often they came only to hear him
say *nada* in their mother tongue.
I found nothing wrong.
To dole out *jarabe* for the children's coughs,
convince the *doña* to stay off that leg.

In his white *saco* Mami ironed out,
smoothing the tired wrinkles
till he was young again,
he spent his days, long days

tending to the ills of immigrants,
his own heart heavy with what was gone,
this new country like a pill
that slowly kills but keeps you
from worse deaths.
What was to be done?

They came to hear him say
nada in their mother tongue.

Queens, 1963

Everyone seemed more American
than we, newly arrived,
foreign dirt still on our soles.
By year's end, a sprinkler waving
like a flag on our mowed lawn,
we were melted into the block,
owned our own mock Tudor house.
Then the house across the street
sold to a black family.
Cop cars patrolled our block
from the Castellucci's at one end
to the Balakian's on the other.
We heard rumors of bomb threats,
a burning cross on their lawn.
(It turned out to be a sprinkler.)

Still the neighborhood buzzed.
The barber's family, Haralambides,
our left side neighbors, didn't want trouble.
They'd come a long way to be free!
Mr. Scott, the retired plumber,
and his plump midwestern wife,
considered moving back home
where white and black got along
by staying where they belonged.
They had cultivated our street
like the garden she'd given up
on account of her ailing back,
bad knees, poor eyes, arthritic hands.
She went through her litany daily.
Politely, my mother listened—
¡Ay, Mrs. Scott, qué pena!
—her Dominican good manners
still running on automatic.
The Jewish counselor next door,
had a practice in her house;
clients hurried up her walk
ashamed to be seen needing.
(I watched from my upstairs window,
gloomy with adolescence,
and guessed how they too must have
hypocritical old world parents.)
Mrs. Bernstein said it was time
the neighborhood opened up.
As the first Jew on the block,
she remembered the snubbing she got
a few years back from Mrs. Scott.
But real estate worried her,
our houses' plummeting value.

She shook her head as she might
at a client's grim disclosures.
Too bad the world works this way.
The German girl playing the piano
down the street abruptly stopped
in the middle of a note.
I completed the tune in my head
as I watched *their* front door open.
A dark man in a suit
with a girl about my age
walked quickly into a car.
My hand lifted but fell
before I made a welcoming gesture.
On her face I had seen a look
from the days before we had melted
into the United States of America.
It was hardness mixed with hurt.
It was knowing she never could be
the right kind of American.
A police car followed their car.
Down the street, curtains fell back.
Mrs. Scott swept her walk
as if it had just been dirtied.
Then the German piano commenced
downward scales as if tracking
the plummeting real estate.
One by one I imagined the houses
sinking into their lawns,
the grass grown wild and tall
in the past tense of this continent
before the first foreigners owned
any of this free country.

New World

I

Tía Ana and Tía Fofi worked at *la factoría*. Tía Fofi attached sleeves to the gaping shoulders. Her specialty was sleeves. But if the Jewish boss, through the Puerto Rican gringa, ordered collars, she did collars, she did buttonholes and panels, stitched darts and pleated gathers. She was a tender-hearted old maid with the sentiments of the married and a sweetheart's pet name, Fofi, for Josefina. She cried often, homesick, *pobrecita* . . . Tía Ana was the serious sister. Her dark eyebrows knotted up like beginner's embroidery. Her hands when she wasn't sewing lay in her lap, praying, one finger capped with a thimble. Tía Ana did the fine needlework, lace collars, shirred bodices, blind stitches only she saw, squinting at the spit-moistened end of the thread she directed into the eye of the needle. They had all come through that eye from Havana, Santiago, San Juan to this United States paradise: old-world seamstresses stitching sleeves to shoulders, yokes to collars, seams holding, skirts flaring like flags unfolding.

II

Tía Ana led Tía Fofi through a maze of subways, three changes and a transfer to the Jamaica Avenue bus station where Mami and I picked them up Saturdays to sew school clothes. We drove the long way home through our nice neighborhood, each lot had a maple blazing in October, a hedge of azaleas blooming in April. We passed house after house after house that looked like ours. Tía Fofi cried, *¡Ya llegamos!* half a dozen times. Tía Ana packed the instructions Mami had written out with a P.S. in English, asking anyone reading this to kindly help our lost aunts. A second P.S. thanked them. At home the aunts pulled doors to be pushed in, reached to the wrong walls for light switches, answered the door when the phone rang. They were dazed with journeys. But their cutting hand was unerring, their stitching strict as a border, their foot steady on the Singer.

III

Tía Ana knew before anyone else that my breasts
had come, that my waist curved in like an hour-
glass. Tía Ana knew that the blood had come
with ghastly stains on the cotton pants she had
made me. But she did not disclose the roundness
of my buttocks, did not whisper to Mami, *This
one is ready to know our secrets.* Did not expose
with a wink or a pat the embarrassing inching
out under my thin undershirt. No, she pinned in
at the waist, out at the hips, stitched secretive
darts, altered old seams, and silently, she let the
new woman in.

IV

Tía Fofi was another story, tattling as she cut,
stitched, seamed and let in hand-me-downs.
Sometimes, pins between pinched lips, she
hemmed in silence. But once gossip got going,
she unpinned her mouth and put in her part, *Fu-
lano had been seen stepping out with Fulana. Fula-
nito would come to no good with Fulanita.* As she
gabbed, the odd cutouts slid under the babbling
Singer and came out cotton jumpers, Sacred
Heart blazers, wash-and-wear blouses. I won-
dered how after decades without a visit to the
island, Tía Fofi knew what wickedness was going
on in her absence. She never told about the man
who had nicknamed her Fofi, left her waiting at
the altar in a gown which had a stitch from every
woman in her hometown. Sometimes she fell si-

lent as she lifted her black-corded glasses and
dabbed each watery eye with one of my practice
handkerchiefs.

V

Papi was the only man around and so it fell to
him to keep up flagging spirits with old world
compliments. Dimpling, Tía Fofi giggled, fid-
dling with her hair, the wispy feminine kind, her
bun always unraveling in helpless black & white
waves down her back. Tía Ana pinned it back up.
Her thin hair behaved itself, the gray strands
packed in a knot and bobbypinned to her skull.
She was partial towards Papi, could recite how
big around was his chest, how many inches from
his shoulders to his wrists. She had mended his
torn pants, fixed his stuck zipper, darned his un-
dergarments intimately. Papi steered wide of her
plain horse face and instead praised her good
health, hard work, and the fact that America
hadn't changed her, she was still Ana García Mo-
rales Perelló Fernández Alfau Pérez Rochet
González.

VI

Mami wanted to invite them to my graduation.
*We're their only family here, and they dressed you all
through school.* It was bad enough having Papi
bowing like the janitor at all my girlfriends' fa-
thers, his fedora at his chest; and bad enough
when Mami looked my girlfriends over, inven-

torying missing buttons, unravelled hems, torn
seams, dirty American habits; without also hav-
ing to bear Tía Ana and Tía Fofi in their best,
old-fashioned, matched outfits, trying out the
few words they knew for American politeness.
On the stage my teachers sat. Each one had
taught me something that would have shocked
my old aunts: Freud and the unconscious, the
gassy origins of the galaxy. The stars and stripes
hung on a pole that was lifted out of its bracket
at the end of our commencement as all of us
stood to sing, *Oh say can you see*, and Tía Ana and
Tía Fofi rose as if they also agreed with what
had become of me.

Sound Bites

First Days

Nueva York, *el hotel* Beverly,
un drugstore in the lobby
(Mami, what is a drugstore?)
a *lavativa* in the window.
Say, hot water bottle, it's nicer.
An elevator, a fire escape.
(What is a fire escape, Mami?)
Up that way, a bad neighborhood.
Is that why we have a doorman?
Or is he protecting our *papi*
from the secret *policía*?
And what is that coming down?
Is it radioactive fallout
from the communists in Cuba?

Is the Virgin's hair falling out?
Ay, Mami, didn't you promise
the USA would be magic?
What else didn't you tell us?

First Year Anniversary

Ay, Mami, what a shame
we came here to be Hispanics
just when the communist Castro
is aiming bombs at Nueva York
and *el presidente* Kennedy
is so worried he has no time
for his little girl Carolina,
who has a pony Macaroni,
and a big house where to keep him,
and her Mami called a *mommie*
wears a little pillbox hat.

Mami's advice

Keep your voices down, girls,
you sound like a hell of a Hesperus,
like birds out of hand, like six of one
and six dozen of the others, you sound
green behind the ears, like a polka
by the fire, you girls are making molehills
by letting sticks and stones hurt you.
They call you spics, what do you care?
It's not in the dictionary, so there.
Speak in your English because
you should do as the Romans do.
Now *cállense la boca y acuéstense.*

I don't want to hear another word.
I don't want to hear another word.

I size up la situación

Translate yourself, *niña,*
you won't last long as you are,
not here in these Estates.
Those tinkertoy legs won't do
or that sorry frizz that says
tatarabuela made a mistake.
You won't last like you are, *chica,*
with your please-to-meet-you personality,
your loud talk of what you miss
on an island these kids never heard of.
Translate your *café con leche*
into a glass of plain milk,
las uñas que te comes y
el de'o que te mamas, nena,
put something else in your mouth,
put English words in your mouth.
Give yourself over, girl,
to the blond, blue-eyed possibilities
so that even as a brown-haired,
olive-skinned spic chick,
you can click with the gringas,
you can jive, you can swing, *¡Epa!*
like you are here on a personal invite
from the United States of America.

Talking back to Mami (years later)

I had to cut myself out
of your paper-doll head,
your speak to me in English,
turn the other cheek when I hit you,
be nice and you'll win them
in the end (like I never did you),
wear a clean slip if you go out,
that way if you have an accident
they'll know you came from a nice family,
not a wetback, a green card alien—
not who you really are.

The Word Made Flesh

I looked up the words
but I could not find them.
I found *breast* and *menstruation*
and *period*—colorless words
for the bright smear on my pants,
the breath breathless in my mouth.
I could not find the real words
for my heart's desire,
for my body's breaking.
There were no words for his smell
or the taste of his sweaty skin
(Island beaches on my tongue)
in the *American Heritage Dictionary*
my parents gave me to ensure
my success in this new language.

I went to the Public Library
to the big fat dictionary,
the one that felt like his weight
on my lap, but I could not find
a word for the rocking on the daybed,
for his tongue like a fish in my mouth.
Only *foreplay* & *intercourse*,
only *privates puberty pudendum*.
None of these words spelled out
my secret I couldn't tell anyone.

I gave up trying to find
his body next to mine,
the small of his back in English.
And I paged through *El Pequeño
Larousse Ilustrado*,
hoping to come upon him
in my first, more heartfelt language,
the accents bearing down
on the sweetly musical syllables,
words rooted in love,
vowels stewing in juices.
But I did not know what to look for
in my deserted childhood Spanish
with Papi still turning the pages
to *la lengua castellana*.

There was no way to say
what I wanted, he wanted,
they did not want me to want,
no way to do it but do it,
lie down and slide my tongue
into his all-American mouth,

looking for the words to say
what was happening in silence
in my *cuerpo* and his heart,
in his *corazón* and my body.

El Round up

Those hard days now called a *background*!
That Babel, now called *bilingual*!
¡Ay, quién sabe! if it wouldn't
have been simpler in Spanish?
But it's over, as when Papi
gave us our vaccinations
for coming to Nueva York,
and we screamed we were dying,
until he said, *¡Ya, se acabó!*
There is nothing left to cry for,
nothing left but the story
of our family's grand adventure
from one language to another.

On Not Shoplifting Louise Bogan's
The Blue Estuaries

Connecticut College, fall 1968

Your book surprised me on the bookstore shelf—
swans gliding on a blueblack lake;
no blurbs by the big boys on back;
no sassy, big-haired picture
to complicate the achievement;
no mentors musing
over how they had discovered
you had it in you
before you even knew
you had it in you.
The swans posed on a placid lake,
your name blurred underwater
sinking to the bottom.

I had begun to haunt
the poetry shelf at the college store—
thin books crowded in by texts,
reference tomes and a spread
of magazines for persistent teens
on how to get their boys,
Chaucer-Milton-Shakespeare-Yeats.
Your name was not familiar,
I took down the book and read.

Page after page, your poems
were stirring my own poems—
words rose, breaking the surface,
shattering an old silence.
I leaned closer to the print
until I could almost feel
the blue waters drawn
into the tip of my pen.
I bore down on the page,
the lake flowed out again,
the swans, the darkening sky.
For a moment I lost my doubts,
my girl's voice, my coming late
into this foreign alphabet.
I read and wrote as I read.

I wanted to own this moment.
My breath came quickly, thinking it over—
I had no money, no one was looking.
The swans posed on the cover,
their question-mark necks arced
over the dark waters.
I was asking them what to do . . .

The words they swam over answered.
I held the book closed before me
as if it were something else,
a mirror reflecting back
someone I was becoming.
The swans dipped their alphabet necks
in the blueblack ink of the lake.
I touched their blank, downy sides, musing,
and I put the book back.

Between Dominica and Ecuador

Between Dominica and Ecuador,
my mother gives a short speech
on violations of human rights,
leaning towards the microphone
as if to whisper the insane facts
above a lightly-sleeping child
while in glass booths overlooking the room
men translate the horrors she tells
into the five official languages.

There is one soldier for every
forty-three persons in the world—
in the voice that said, *Drink your milk,*
with the look that warned, *Watch your step!*
—but only one doctor for every

one thousand and thirty people.
I switch the dial to Russian,
French, English, Chinese,
until I've dialed her voice again:
Todos los días 14,000 niños
mueren de malnutrición . . .
The starving children who haunted
my childhood meals resurrect,
hovering over the meeting room,
wailing babies from Grenada,
Seychilles, Bangladesh, China,
Somalia, India, Costa Rica.
My mother no longer concerned
with using them for her threats
champions their right to fill
their stomachs with our excess.

Beside her with her eyes
unmistakably in my face,
I scan the room for reactions,
picking out those countries
guilty of her sad facts.
The delegates from Salvador—
plump playboys in business suits—
earphones off, heads together,
proofread their declaration,
denials piling up like the dead.
The beauty from Bangladesh
sorts through her stack of memos
while at Lebanon's delegation
two made-up women giggle
over some private joke.
Kampuchea is absent;

absent, too, the South African delegate.
I cannot find the United States.
Nervous countries predominate,
Nicaragua and Haiti,
Iraq, Israel, Egypt.
A young attaché from Iran
hands out personalized copies
of a speech to be delivered
by His Excellency Mahallati.
In the name of God, I read,
The Compassionate, the Merciful.
I'm half listening to my mother
rounding up with how the cost
of one Trident sub could pay
for immunizing our newborns
against six lethal diseases.

Behind me I hear the pages
of a newspaper crackling open.
I turn around to a dark mustache
from a country I never heard of,
eyes perusing a foreign paper
of fresh, untranslated horrors.
I wither him with a gaze,
turn back to my mother,
a nervous, white-haired girl
who has gone on reading her speech,
Every minute a newborn dies.
The past recedes before us;
my own grievances against her—
a whipping with a hair brush,
a half hour locked in a closet,
a denied touch in a dark hour—

seem now inconsequential
before this universal arsenal.
For moments I almost forgive her
until I hear her winding up
with the tone of ultimatum,
If you want love you must earn it!

She thanks everyone for listening,
hopes the world will be better.
Then turns to me and whispers,
How was I? her face flushed
with terror of public speaking.
You were perfect, I lie the truth
I still yearn to hear from her.
Smiling, she seems untouched
by the horrors she has summoned.
In the glassy booths above us,
the earphoned guardians click off
the Dominican Republic.

Beginning Again

Sometimes I wake up in the middle of the night
counting over our losses again.

But if on a warm afternoon in late March,
stopping the car to trespass in a stubble field,

wearing my sister's hand-me-down sweater,
looking back to the road where I left the car parked,

if I can let it all go: the house since sold
to strangers, the four girls in matching dresses

descending into the windy runway,
their homeland a cloudshape on a map,

if the losses, the wrong answers
(some painfully lived out),

if these are not so deeply grieved in the heart-
broken mind so that we cannot possibly recover,

so that we are always descending
into a city of strangers, always forcing

our tongues to shape the foreign word
for what we *really* mean, then all of us,

and I mean the whole world, can be saved.
I know that sounds like a schoolgirl talking,

a bit self-indulgent, I know there are men
with large salaries, men with kempt hair

and tidy, monosyllabic mouths, men
I have yearned for in the impersonal way

of young girls towards a god or a rockstar,
who would smile, fondling the change in their pockets

at this vision. But if the deepest loss,
short of death—of a language, of the valuable

codes of the mind, of a land dusty with ancestors—
can be, not just survived, but made into the matter

of hope, made into song, not into a hatchet
to cut off the offending parts, made into poems,

then blessed be the end of things, the loss of whatever
secures us blindly and mutely to our lives.

If in late March as I walk in a field, I let it all go,
the mourning, the holding on—

then briefly, as if for the first time,
the world untold, loved as never before,

the self beginning itself again, the field
heading for spring, the seeds sown,

the grasses bending, the car pointing
towards the horizon I'll call home.

—*for Tita*

Making Up the Past

This never happened and yet I want the memory
so much I have made it true, recalling

a fall day our third year (and a month)
in this country: the house recently bought

in a nice neighborhood, my sisters and I paired up
in the two immaculate bedrooms that look out

into the sad box of a backyard, a yard
I will wander in all my long adolescence

searching for answers that will never be there
in the tidy oak (my sister says maple)

and the scrappy bushes of something
that never did well in the shade.

The memory or rather pseudo memory
is of my mother in a bathrobe at the window

watching my progress down the block
and around the corner until I am out of sight,

not knowing (how could she know?)
and knowing (she always knows everything!)

of my terror at setting off by myself
to Hillside to pick up something she needs.

I'm pretending to myself and to her that my fear
is really excitement, that I want to be

adrift in America without her,
that if by the time I head back

the ground gives, the streets shift
(I am sure this will happen),

and I cannot find her up the hill
of our driveway at the bay of little windows,

why then, I'll survive, an ethnic Dorothy
(my first beloved American movie)

who never gets back to her Mami in Kansas
but gets caught up in the rest of her life.

This is how my memory ends my childhood,
with a made-up moment of my mother

in a flowered bathrobe she never owned,
the zipper fixed twice already

from my mother's roughhandling
(always in a hurry), her hands lifting

though even with the tints of memory
I can't touch up the gesture as goodbye

(she is checking a smudge on the glass),
a memory doublecoded in Spanish

so that I also remember *Mami*
acechándome por la ventana.

What could possess me to invent this?
As if we need to stage our losses,

set the lights just so, dress our mothers
like dolls in clothes we make up for them,

and then rewind to the moment of departure,
the kiss at the door, the query, *Do you have*

enough money? the click of the latch, the jingling
of the chain lock sliding back in its groove.

Even now when I know half a dozen ways
to get back to that mock Tudor house

on a hillock of landfill, even now
I can make myself feel lost all over again,

feel that thirty years have passed in which
all I've been doing is reading street signs

for a way back to a moment that never
(I am sure of it) happened. So be it—

this movie we must make of the past
so it doesn't break our hearts,

or worse, leave us, in remembering it,
leave us, untouched and dismissive, turning

the pages of our albums, reading the captions
to what we can prove really happened—

which will never be this moment I made up
of my mother's hand lifting, my steady progress

down the block, my shoulders already set
in a posture I assume every time

I sit down to write—a feisty, terrified squaring
of the shoulders—my hands fisting

in my pockets and all of me refusing
(for the moment) to turn back and face

what I am leaving behind, what I must know
I will keep coming back to all my imagined life.

—for David Huddle

IV

The Joe Poems

First Love Letter

Julia Altagracia María Teresa Alvarez
c/o Yarnall
Wings Point
Vermont
05445

                                        Dearest—
Addressed by your hand the envelope seems
posted from an earlier century.
My full name I divulged to you one night
looks like an old title, the letters jeweled,
the accents—extra ones!—like music notes:
it's a wonder somebody didn't steal the mail
from the old postbox at the end of the path.
I take the letter on my daily walk, trespassing
through the deserted lakefront lawns
of the summer people, already gutsier
for your letter in my jacket pocket, already
transformed by your calligraphy
into a sad, beautiful heroine
living with her best girlfriend between jobs,

between great loves that have moved her
here and there in the name of love.
                    The heroine roams the fields
under the high blue skies of late September.
See her in her black silks go pacing by,
headed toward the point where locals tell
there've been a couple of hardluck suicides.
Let's hope the wise Yarnall into whose care
our heroine's consigned will come in time
to coax her from the gleaming rocks below
with a warm shawl and a steaming cup of tea.
That's how you make me feel when I receive
your scripted envelope, the off-white paper
like starched linens on a curtained bed,
the heft of the packet slightly heavier
than regular mail, my head light . . .
until I tear the envelope only to read
the mundane news of your everyday life.
(*Finished the watercolors for the children's book,*
Jennifer's had a bad cold for a week,
builders began work on the new house.)
Disappointed, I watch the gulls wheeling
above the lake in the near shapes of letters
like the scattered alphabet I've carried in my head
this long year of my not being able to write.
I used to think them beautiful background birds
until I read somewhere they're scavengers
who flock to landfills trilling their greedy cries.
Oh, what a heap of trashy fantasy
and purple prose of romance fills my head—
I, who have learned of love mostly from books I love!
My Romeos, Heathcliffs, my Anthonys,
like rich brocaded tapestries

hiding you from my view, whoever *you* are.
My cautious heart tempered by irony
and far too many heady heartbreaks
knows this will never do for daily love.
Where was it I read recently the phrase,
*the healing beauty of everything that is
commonplace*? Some book I love, no doubt.
My dear, let us be plain and simple with each other,
talk high Romance, but then come down to earth,
the right place for love, the poet I love sayeth.
I roam the woods and fields and pebbled shore,
the brief, make-believe heroine of Wings Point,
glad enough with the beauty of this spot
my good friend Yarnall lives on,
glad also that your printed words have drawn
words from my silence like doves from a hat,
most glad as I refold the heavy sheet
back in its envelope emblazoned with
my name made gorgeous by your gifted hand
to have as antidote upon my lips
your common-sounding, no less cherished name—

Joe.

Touchstone

After so many deaths, I live and write;
I once more taste the dew and rain
and relish versing.

—GEORGE HERBERT, *"The Flower"*

At La Guardia's touch-tone, charge-a-call phone
        I dial your number,
                missing you,
and over & above that loss,
        minutes before boarding,
            I discover
I've lost a word,
        can't come up with it at all,
            that awful blank in my head
        I know so well
as if the whole necklace of sense had snapped—
        the letters of our names tumbling
            on the floor,
                a random alphabet,
anonymous as the faces
        that surround me here,

so far from you.
I brave the heavily instruction-plated phone,
          insert my card,
                    hear buzzes, tones,
then ringing
          I pray won't be
                    an operator scolding
          that I did things wrong.
Your daughter answers,
          then you come on,
                    and for *hello*
I have to laugh
          it worked!
          reaching you
minutes before taking off
          into a night sky
          blank
                    as a just-washed blackboard.
It's a bad connection, your voice
          tinny with static,
                    tiny
                              as make-believe,
while all around me
          the drone and babble
          of strangers.
You ask, *Can you hear me?*
          Yes, I say,
                    and then, since death
          could be so soon
and you're so far away,
          I say the ache inside of me all day,
                    I miss you.
What's more, I've lost a word

and so feel even more
            at odds.
And now—through the crackling wire—
            I feel your interest sparkle
                        like the starry sky
            I wished for flying,
your love of words as keen,
                        as quick,
            as genuine as mine.
Is there a word for a stone
            you hold things to
            to see if they are genuine?
And instantly, as if you stood
            beside me
                        in the echoing terminal
and brushed your hand,
            your bookmaker's artist-fingers,
                        every one,
upon the palette of my upper back,
            you say the word
                        that I was searching for,
touchstone?
                        Touchstone! I echo,
            moved to find it
                        true to my recollection,
Touchstone,
            brushed of its dusty muteness
                        by your voice.
My shoulders give,
            my breath comes
            easefully.
Touchstone, I keep saying it over,
            touchstone,

                    touchstone,
feeling that tears are coming,
                because I recognize
            this ache again
                        for words, for love,
a man's tongue dumb
                inside my mouth—
            Name it! Name it!
                you're always saying.
After a year of silence,
            the words,
                the words are surfacing,
wanting my recollecting,
            my tongue,
                my breath,
on account of your loving agency
            (*Name it! Name it!*)
                as now on the phone
            you pleasure me
with the word I had on the tip
            of my tongue,
                touchstone!
as if we were together again
            on the hotel bed,
                finger to finger,
                    palms,
chests, bellies, hips,
                thighs, legs,
                    feet to feet,
all the length
            of our absent
                imagined bodies
genuinely touching.

Going Back to Sleep

After making love, I hear you in the bathroom:
        the snap of the light switch,
the tap of the toilet seat as you lift it up—
        a glad sign a man is in the house.
Your ready pee phrases a steady patter
        in the clear bowl of water,
the hesitant ticklish drip of the finish,
        the imagined sigh
as you lean forward, flush, a great flourish
        of water cuing me
to curl back to the shape of your body,
        returning. But no,
you linger in the bathroom, and suddenly
        I am wide awake
as to what I might have left out in the open

that I do not want you to see,
the place in our knowing still the beginning
        of the love story,
hero and heroine dressed up in their best behavior;
        neither of us yet ready
for the plot to turn, old selves shed like our clothes
        at the foot of the bed;
neither of us yet ready for what we have discussed,
        what our creaturely bodies
have already risked, brief as they know
        they are. And I hear
the distinct clink of the medicine cabinet
        coming unlatched
as you pull away your own face in the mirror,
        looking for more of me
than I've disclosed in the dark safety
        of the bedroom,
the secret creature on the white tin shelves
        of her toilet,
the floss in its locket-type box, silly cakes
        in their compacts
with my heightened complexion, little bottles
        of desyrel, dalmane—
O my, O my, what will you make of me?
        I lean over the edge of the bed,
ashamed at the thought of you
        on the brink of knowing me,
your hands cupped at the very quick of me . . .
        O my, O my.
I reach down for the comforting touch
        of your soiled clothes:
the eager tangle of your shorts, the sad impotence
        of the empty pant legs.

I pull your shirt to my face, smell you,
   released on the cloth
like a pungent Veronica, trust you again,
   entrust myself to you again
as if only the flesh knows how to keep faith
   with the critical, wandering Other,
whom I hear now, closing the cabinet door,
   lingering a moment
before your own face in the mirror,
   your good reasons
not to love, before you're drawn back
   into your tired body,
the familiar curves of your arms, the small
   rough palms,
the broad plane of your chest where the heart
   knocks and knocks
at a door that I hope is open. O my, O my,
   O my sleepy love,
our breathing falls in together, we lie
   in each other's arms,
all night we go back and forth, back and forth,
   towards what we think we want.

Bookmaking

*Words, let water from an unseen infinite ocean
come into this place as energy for the dying
and even the dead.*

—RUMI

At the Pierpont Morgan I go up and down
    the glass cases of the East Room,
studying bindings, toolings, papercutting,
    as if by learning your craft,
I will know you in the books exposed before me,
    the thick seams clasping
the packets together the way your hand will
    fold around my forearm,
your urgent fingers whitening my skin
    as if to bind us in a certain moment
of knowing; the pearled vellum lucent
    as lovemaking; the leather covers
pockmarked in a scarred masculine pattern
    as if we undressesd hastily
and your jacket's rough tweed pressed

against my leg as you bore down,
parting me, the way I've seen you take
    a book in both hands, parting
its thick wedge of pages to the exact passage
    you want me to read.
I go slowly over each display, accustoming myself
    to this new way of looking
at books: gold leaf, embossed crescents, Dove's
    versus Zaehendorf's bindings.
I read each legend card carefully
    as if to know you better
without the distraction of your body
    beside my body,
the vocabulary of your craft still odd on my tongue
    like the taste of you at first,
an uncertain pleasure, the self posed between
    its celibate single-mindedness
and its being cracked open with the creaking give
    of a new binding in a book you've made.
I study them now—books we've both loved
    with a passion almost of the body:
Leaves of Grass, The Marriage of Heaven and Hell,
    To the Lighthouse, changed utterly
as I pass by, taking each one in, marveling.
    Now they have become objects:
the filigreed leaves closed into solid gold,
    the leather covers tooled
into splendid, intricate beds of flowers.
    Now they have become
texts, tomes, volumes—books I would touch
    were they not encased
in their carefully monitored boxes
    for the generations to come.

Now the words become flesh,
    your body, my body,
side by side in my small twin bed.
    I lean over, closer,
clouding the glass with my frank breath,
    wanting you,
the idea of you no longer enough to hold me
    until the next time we meet,
the body keen to the hunger you have awakened.
    I lean forward for the righting touch
of the physical world, the dark warm wood
    of the case gleaming with polish.
Now, I am knowing my body, late
    into its fourth decade,
in the passionate way you have known it:
    the seam of the spine
centered in the jacket of the shoulders,
    the ligaments tooled on the plates
of the clavicles, the legible bones
    of the wrists and the ankles.
And my breath comes quickly for time
    seems suddenly short
for all the knowing of the body
    of the world, the touching
all the body of the world, and the handing down
    to the generations to come
the world's body loved by our passionate arts.

Anatomy Lesson

A hundred drums are being beaten in our hearts—
the sound might reach us tomorrow.

—RUMI

We are sitting in bed, my legs on your lap,
        my head to your side
on the pillow you have trussed behind it—
        as always lovingly
mindful of the body. It starts simply
        with your pointing out
the tibia on my leg, the gastrocnemius—I ask you
        to spell, the ulna
and radius of my forearm: how one contracts
        as the other lets go,
when suddenly we are launched into
        the sacrament of conversation
—everything we say transformed by a certain
        kind of attention
into metaphor, words crystallizing all we've lived

into a healing meaningfulness,
so we know who we are again, and for this,
　　　yes, I could love you . . .
We all want, you admit, beginning
　　　a sign of the cross,
touching your forehead, your heart,
　　　but then, instead of your shoulders,
descending to touch your crotch, *to put*
　　　all three together with someone,
a near impossibility, and we're damn lucky
　　　if we get this & this,
or this & that. You semaphore all possible
　　　combinations of two,
while sadly I watch your fingers spiderwebbing
　　　the air between us,
knowing that we haven't yet made
　　　that blessed triple connection,
crystallizing all we are into One, one body,
　　　heart & soul. O my love,
do not remind me how our bodies withheld
　　　from each other last night,
tense with desire & lack of desire, a mixed bag,
　　　and the bed too narrow.
As if we had already achieved
　　　such passionate affection,
we wisely kept back from risking it all
　　　for that fantasy
of all three needs met by one person:
　　　a soulmate for the godless.
Let that god die! you say, *and let's just enjoy*
　　　whatever we have with each other.
You pull my arm towards you,
　　　explaining arboreal articulation:

how the radius swivels as the hand grabs hold
      and releases its purchase.
Our high talk turns wistful this late afternoon,
      the light falling
in latticework patterns, I in my panties
      and socks & camisole—
since you like the room cold, and you
      in your bare skin
and thick bottle glasses, adjusted
      every now & then
as I move in & out of the range of your
      nearsighted vision.
I am saddened by your talk,
      by the long night's dissatisfaction
I want you to say was all right
      as we touch now
sweetly like sisters, measuring palms,
      you like the clever one,
explaining our lessons:
      how every seven years
we replace all but the cells of the brain
      and the spine,
so that at thirty-seven I've cast off five bodies
      and am inside my sixth,
how you're in your seventh
      at forty-seven.
I think of them all, ghosts we have brought
      along with us:
the boy you once were—pulling the pigtails
      of my first body's hair;
the good schoolgirl of my second body
      raising her hand

to tell on your third body's mischief;
      my third body clowning
as you withdrew into your pensive fourth;
      the beauty I came into
in my fourth body, if I could have given her
      to you, if your fifth body
could have held her for solace those years
      you were hard at work,
raising your girls, overwhelmed by the end
      of your first true-love story.
Or if my frantic fifth could have lain down eased
      by your humanized sixth.
Oh, my sweet seventh, how many lives together
      haven't we already missed!
You are right to stop my sixth's passionate
      reach towards your seventh,
my wanting all of you to know all of me—
      so much has already *not* happened
that perhaps to be here, together,
      talking away this sweet while
is all a body can ask for?
      As now, in your diagram
of muscles & bones, you sketch a little boat
      afloat on a scallop of waves
to show how our arms work like a mast
      balanced by mainstays.
See how we must live, see how we must love—
      giving & taking—
not expecting too much? My radius swivels,
      my ulna gives,
I lay down my hand between your sternum
      and solar plexus

to feel the one muscle you haven't yet touched on
      in your explanations,
nor I yet touched down upon from
      my high expectations.

Monkey Business

Male behavior perplexed me from the start. . . .
After years observing baboons, I see them as
intelligent manipulators . . . even without
language as we know it. Humans, of course,
have taken these traits to new heights.

—SHIRLEY STRUM, *National Geographic,*
    November, 1987

You send me to read the latest
        National Geographic,
an article on baboons, primarily
        about male behavior
vis à vis mating: who gets what
        female and why.
I'll read it, hoping to understand
        your baffling behavior,
which male friends claim is unmale-like,
        which women friends
warn is a sign *that guy's just out*
        for a good time.
You advise me—and I quote you—
        Flourish! (Good advice.)
Don't take yourself—or me—
        too seriously. (Fair.)

Take other lovers, that way you won't
        feel too neglected
when I can't come through for you.
        What about that guy
who speaks Spanish? He sounds simpatico.
        Or the photographer
with the bad temper who snapped your photo?
        Give him a second chance.

On my end of the phone, my jaw
        unhinges, reptile-like,
my blood runs cold as an amphibian's.
        Is the man human?
We banter; I trying to keep the frog
        of disappointment
from my throat, my Adam's apple
        riding up and down
with swallowing the forbidden fruit
        of wanting (only) you.

Next day, I stop in at the library,
        sit at the window seat
overlooking the village green
        (schoolchildren kicking
homeward through the leaves)
        reading the magazine.
Athletic-looking baboons romp
        through the Kenyan veldt.
The males—who look just like the females
        to me—mystified
the female anthropologist who spent
        ten years observing them.

Goodbye, she writes, *to the old male-*
               aggression theory!
The males who got the females were
               the slow and patient ones,
who practised guile rather than
               exercised brute force,
who traveled, rested, took their time
               getting to know the females
rather than pushy types who dropped in
               only when the heat was on.
For proof, pages and pages of *National*
               Geographic glossies show
the monkeyshines of the Pumphouse Gang:
               Here's handsome Antonio
coming on strong with grunts and lipsmacks
               while the oblivious Zelda
snacks on the fleshy roots of sansevieria
               the shy Gargantua tenders her.
Pretty Theodora lets herself go
               in the Kenyan hay
with peace-loving Strider while Dr. Bob
               exposes sharp canines,
making his "threat face," unremarked.
               Frieda, rosy-rumped
from her last pregnancy, enjoys the sun
               warm on her backside
with baby Teleki and male friend Ron
               while peeved Pinocchio
picks a fight in a fold-out sequence,
               which ends, bottom right,
with Ron minding baby Teleki
               while pissed off Mom
flashes her hot-pink bottom at P's nose.

Below, on the green
a team of boys and tomboys kick
        a soccerball around.
A tiny girl, a braid plaited so tightly
        down her back
one fears its unraveling as if it were
        the stitching on a doll,
enters the reading room, unpacks
        her homework
and tongue out, arm at a crippling
        angle, pencils
in a laborious hand her capital
        and lowercase alphabets.
Downstairs, the phone rings:
        someone wants to know
if the latest book on how-to not-to
        love too much is in.
It's out. There's a wait on it.
        Another late fall afternoon
in the human race.

        I think of you
back at your studio—that time of day
        the light falls
just-so on your drawing board.
        You cap your pens,
lid inks, write in your daybook
        today's accomplishments,
have your first drink, begin making
        dinner for your girls,
perhaps—given your mood—give me a call:
        So, how's life treating you?

Any developments in the dark-room
            department?
Today I'm not home to sass back, *No!*
            I'm at the library
doing some background reading
            the better to understand
your monkeying around!
                The slow Gargantua
closes in on Zelda, Ron folds up
            snugly beside Frieda,
Pinocchio sulks—the Pumphouse Gang
            goes back
to the magazine rack as cries
            from down below
rise up with the current no-win score.
            My little wordsmith friend
contorts her body over a capital *M*.
            I watch her wistfully,
thinking back on the article's remark:
            what most distinguishes
her from Teleki, say, or you from Ron,
            or me from Zelda
is this bittersweet accomplishment,
            words that explain
but often complicate with more
            elaborate art
the monkey business of the human heart.

The Last Love Story

Don't grieve.
Anything you lose comes round
in another form.

— Rumi

After you tell me
            your last love story
        we lie in bed, listening
to the random late-night traffic
            as if we were waiting
        for the rumble
            of a specific motor.
The streetlight through
        the half-opened blinds
            bars you up & down
the length of your sad body
        in a cage of light.
            I open its little door
        —wide—

put my hand in, wanting
    to take something of you
        in my palms
    and soothe it.
But the cage is empty,
    nothing, not a word,
        not a note.
And suddenly, I know
    you have gone back
        to that restaurant,
the steam from your untouched dinner
    vanishing
        into the dark hole
    of your opened mouth
as you lean over your plate
        hearing the news
    she has just now told you.
I lie very still
    so as not to intrude
        on the two of you.
She tells you, you repeat
    what she tells you,
    your voice—I can tell—
        about to break.
The tiny clinks of silver & glasses
    at the tables
        around you
like the frantic sound
    of your hand singling
        key after key
    in a keyring,
looking for the one

that will let you back
    inside the life
you two have shared together.
You know they are in there:
    the fabulous pair,
        male & female,
with their wild gold and opalescent
    blue feathers,
        their bright crests,
    their pearly beaks,
creatures no one
        but you & she
    have ever been.
You shake your head, *No!*
    as if to clear your vision of them
        beyond the door
    she has just now closed.
You go back to her promises,
        vows like vigorous fires
    she once lighted,
now only the ashy craters
    of old campfires.
        I lie beside you,
    helpless as you are helpless,
your hands lying
    on either side of your plate
        as if you were going
    to offer it to her,
as if you could lure her back
    with little delicacies,
        birdseed,
    pieces of pink melon.

The table before you
        seems suddenly cluttered
                with incongruous
        platters & baskets.
You are baffled by this plenty;
        you want to get up
                and go outside,
        breathe in the frosty night,
connect the dots of old stars
        into the fabulous
                new creature
        you alone will become.
But you sit there
        as if you were still
                locked
        in this moment of parting.
I lie beside you,
        troubled
        as to what to do.
I reach down
        my hands
                into that restaurant.
I close the little door,
        latch it
        from the outside,
take away the platters,
        the wine
                and the water.
I want you to die
        to your life together,
                to burn to ashes
        in that old fire,

then rise
      like my own phoenix
          from the man you were
to the lover you are
      in spite of yourself
          again becoming.

Missing Missives

In Fellini's *Amarcord*, the idiot
        middle-aged cousin
is taken out for a picnic by his kin,
        and just before going home,
the fellow clambers up a giant tree
        bawling away
into the dusty gold Italian dusk,
        I want a woman!
I want a woman! And won't come down
        despite all pleas
until—as I remember it—a memory
        you mustn't trust as fact
since we both know how apt I am
        to make my stories up—
a great Jacob-size ladder's propped

against that tree,
and up goes the wild-haired kissing cousin
          to fetch her lunatic blood.
Shirtwaist unbuttoned to her waist,
          she lures him down,
rung by lusty rung, to safe ground,
          where beefy uncles
nab him, chuckling, and conduct him
          home to the asylum.

Last night over the phone I put my plate
          on the table,
famished by your week-long silence,
          the postbox, tongue out,
like an empty mouth. *I want a man!*
          I want a man!
All this talk of friendship is making me
          nervous, all this exchange
of failed love stories is making me
          sad and anxious,
all this distance is making me horny!
          Your laughter's short
and through your nose, a sign, I know,
          you're caught off guard.
"But we *are* friends, and that in a month's time
          is a minor miracle!"
Jesus, I smart, *if all you want's a friendship,*
          fine! Go pal with gals,
go dally with Sallys! I want a man,
          you understand?
This time your laughter's genuine.
          "Ditto!" you say.
"I'm wanting too, I want a woman,

I want you!
But stop your needling mind from stitching
        together a sampler
of negative reasons why I haven't called!
        I've been busy, that's all."
We settle into that tone that means
        we're comfortable again,
exchange an edited week's worth of news,
        ending with your request
that I not misconstrue your silences
        but trust the ways in which
you take your risks—though silence seems
        (I don't say this)
shortshrifting the love end of the stick.

        The next day on my walk,
I take a different turn and end up in a sunny field
        of milkweed pods:
some rattling empty husks, some still shut
        snugly like cocoons,
many at half-spilled stages
        that the blowing wind
of late October launches in my direction,
            milkweed missiles,
seedlings dangling from silken parachutes.
        My hand yearns
towards a still-packed pocket. I truss
        my fingers in,
scoop out the whole battalion,
        then remembering last night's call,
your laughter, mine, our simple needs
        that get mixed up
with all our talk about relationships,

and can't be met
by silences or reassurances
        over the longing distances—
I unbutton my jacket, hold wide the flaps
        and let the seedlings
coat my sweater and sweat pants—as if
        they were missiles
in your maneuvers of desire and fear;
        as if they were missals
that could renew my loss of faith
        in loving at our age;
as if, I say, as if they were the many
        many missing missives
you haven't time to sit & write,
        although a dozen
dozen times a day you post them from
        your thoughts,
your heart, your lips, your loins
        to me—or so you say.

Staying Up Alone

I don't have any trouble with my child,
but my girl and heroine give me
a hell of a time!

—a participant at a woman's workshop

I'd hate to think that after all our hard work
to grow up and be ready to love,
the world is full of men who prefer
their women as girls.

—a journal entry

After a week apart we sit face to face
    at the kitchen table,
I no longer daughterly and draped
    across your lap,
but fiercer, womanly, a stranger
    neither of us knows too well:
Red Riding Wolf, as I've grown
    to call her after the popular book
about the inner wild women
    who run with the wolves.
So far, mine hasn't made
    much progress,
each time she sets off on her own,
    the girl inside her tires,
the child whines for home,

the heroine wants her hero,
and all of me ends up
    in bed with you!
This time I've come to talk
    of my transformation,
unsure if it will hold
    under the first bold look
of your wanting me back.
    But you—exhausted
by All Hallow's Eve when you
    dressed up as a werewolf
but got sick as a dog
    from too much drinking
and had to be driven home—
    keep nodding off,
apologizing by way
    of your slapdash story
of yesterday's drunk for tonight's
    disappointing rendez-vous.
But this new woman smiles,
    touches your cheek
still smudged with werewolf black,
    says, *That's all right*,
although the girl is petulant
    and the heroine checks
her watch for the exact hour
    at which her hero
turned into the man slumped
    in the chair before her.
But this strange woman waits,
    not spelled by the alphabet
of who you want her to be,

        solid, incisive, heartfelt,
damn good company! She's heard
        of your recent silences;
she knows how the story goes,
        that passion pales
and most of the rest of love
        is luck and a sense of timing.
But still, the young girl yearns
        for the smiley face
of your good behavior,
        and the troubled heroine pouts
at the villain's grin
        of your jack-o'-lantern
that proves she has grounds
        to sink into depression,
and the child pleads
        for her Cinderella story.
But the stranger turns
        from such grade-school fantasies
to help you climb the stairs to bed,
        your arm draped on her shoulder—
the heroine cringing, seeing it still
        as the werewolf paw,
and the girl alarmed she has to sleep
        with the big bad creep
of the fairytale who tried
        to eat her up.
You sleep in the barred light
        of the canted blinds,
an imprisoned man.
        She sits on the dark edge
of your king-size bed

pondering the legend
of the man turned wolf
    you became last night.
Lycanthropy, it's called
    (she looked it up
in your bedside dictionary):
    a man's ability
to be transformed into an animal
    is a common belief,
although what the animal is
    depends upon
which is the most powerful
    & feared animal
in a particular locality.
    The girl looks down
at your sleeping face and sees
    the frightening beast
of the Russian steppes,
    and the heroine gasps
at this sorry understudy
    who has dared to play
the true love in her story.
    And her eyes snap shut
like those of a doll laid back
    on a child's bed.
Then, the child sleeps, the girl sleeps,
    the heroine sleeps,
and you sleep, the head & heart
    of that puppy-love pack.
And left alone, keeping vigil
    over the sleeping form
of your masquerade as man,

it's me—transformed
into the most feared and powerful
    and lonesome animal
in this locality—a grown woman.

You Remember the Definitions,
Not the Words

Part of me wants to eat the stones
and hold you back when you're leaving.

—RUMI

After that first grand month of passion
            and wild hope
we turn back to our single beds
            pensive a moment
like young girls not yet sure
            how the future works.
How is it our loved bodies
            slipped through our bodies,
leaving behind the overweight man
            and the too-thin woman
you and I have become again
            for each other?
Our last overnight I found myself
            alone in your bed
and tracked you downstairs

to your studio
where you pleaded insomnia, indigestion,
            hell! old age and more.
That *more* has kept me up these many nights
            trying to readjust my sights
to another love turned friend,
            struggling to give myself
to my own life again—as I was wont to do
            before you came
rekindling passion in my heart for words
            made flesh, flesh fluent
with the verbs of touching, long nights
            palavering through
the thick and thin of our two bodies.
            Estranged by weeks now
of your silence I do not call and ask
            what's happening—
I've read the end in your distracted gaze
            cooled since that first night,
yea! our laughter ringing in my little room
            you like Adam naming everything,
aghast at my Eve-like appetite
            for the fruits of your tongue.

In my walks these days I smell winter
            unwrapping its winds,
a camphor smell, an icy piney tinge
            on everything,
the trees all bare, abandoned nests clumped
            sadly on the boughs.
The cones and milkweed pods disperse
            their future generations
propelled by hopeful hooks & whirligigs

& parachutes:
next year's maples nothing right now
                but gadgetry.

Next time we talk, you find me so
                subdued & sad,
you reach for the ready remedy:
                some words you say
you've been saving to send me
                "one of these days,"
the phrase so elegiac I cringe
                from my usual pleasure
of your putting words in my mouth.
                But when I ask for them,
you remember only the definitions,
                not the words,
your mouth empty like the sorrowing
                who have no words
to link the baffling happenings
                of the world
into a meaningful sequence:
                the story of their lives.
Give me the definitions then, I ask,
                and in a rush they come—
a word for lizard-like, a word
                for the indentation
between the nose & upper lip,
                a word for to fill
to satisfaction, to prevent
                the waste or loss of.
Yes, I say, after each one,
                as if they were the seeds

of the coming spring, the brittle pod
        unsnapping
the spiraling green, the hopeful inching
        towards being!
Already solace is springing
        in my heart,
the poems of our trying
        to talk ourselves in love.

Home Fires

Our last full day together we pass a house
    that has just burned down,
the heap still smoldering in the autumn sun,
    nothing left standing
but for an absurd fireplace—a hearth
    without a home—
while firemen in their rubber boots
    and hats and coats,
ludicrous garb this Indian summery day,
    coil their hoses up
and one with a clipboard goes around
    adding up the ruin.
The death of a house is a sad, sad thing,
    you sigh, but I
who've never known a home

                since childhood to lose
think of another loss to mourn
                and touch your arm,
the thigh already seeming a slight trespass.
        Beyond the absent house
that would have blocked the view,
                the maples blaze,
red and gold. *High autumn*, I name it
                to distract you
for we've just come from visiting the site
                of your new house:
nothing but cleared-up ground,
                lathe and string,
and your believing hand signaling
                a studio, kitchen, den,
where I see only devastated woods,
                uprooted maples, birches,
their grotesque roots exposed
                        like frantic spiders
grappling in the air for missing webs.
        It's past high autumn,
you say, *a tinge past glorious.*
        Spindly trees
my eye had missed until
                you point them out
now mar the masterpiece stretched
                on your windshield
driving home, your words like omens
                on my tongue:
The peak is gone—of the season.

        That night we lie awake
making—what you call—talking love,

103

         middle-aged lovers
catching each other up
         on each one's history
of love and loss:
         yours on a firm foundation
of houses, daughters, a body of work.
         Mine, a kite's tail
of addresses, the penciled entry
         in my friends' phonebooks,
the airborne Chagall gal
         needing to come back
down to earth, briefly to love
         a man in the flesh,
make brief flesh of our flesh,
     '   bone of brief bone,
briefly to sing a briefly lasting song—
         needs you don't share
just coming out from under family;
         the new house
built for a single, solitary man.

         —Across the bed,
we look towards where we sense
         the other's eyes
but see only the darkness between us,
         speaking in whispers now
as if to ourselves, you saying how
         you mean to compensate
the damage done at the construction site
         by making wreaths
of all the cut-down trees and burying them
         in the foundation:
a horrid thought, I think, to vault

those living things
under your feet, a thought I don't share
        already sensing
your defensiveness. We say, *Goodnight,*
        *Good*night,
only a suffix's difference from *Goodbye.*

        . . . Hours later
I wake from a bad dream, unsure
        of where I am.
I touch your thigh, the great beam
        of your spine,
the broad support of shoulderblades,
        and hear again
my nightmare's sounds of roots ripping,
        tendrils tearing
as when you yank a coverlet of moss
        from its damp bed,
that sound turned up of flames roaring
        when the timbers catch,
the great house gives, the edifice falls down!
        I listen to your breathing
for the comfort that it gives,
        breathe in, breathe out,
trying to match my breathing to your breath,
        briefly in time
as if we could combine our lives and blow
        this ending out.

V

The Other Side
El Otro Lado

The Other Side/*El Otro Lado*

I

I drove up in Mami's Mercedes, the uniformed guard waved me in
before I could explain the car was only on loan for a week,
I didn't know how to work the alarm or turn on the high beams—
he was trained to admit white women riding in silver chariots.
As the weeks went by and I darkened, hiking midday in the sun,
refusing lifts from Tropical Tours or from rummy businessmen
stopping their canopied golf carts to ask where I was from,
and hey, was it hot enough for me? As the weeks went by,
the guards began checking my card to make sure I belonged.

There were five of us all together for this winter's residency:
one, a Parisian working with large canvases and no patience
with the colony's handyman who didn't know how to stretch them;
another, a globe-trotting German, who arrived fully equipped

with her young lover and vegetable juicer, who drew "automatically"—
a Ouija board sort of thing—her hand directed to sketch
primordial ancestor figures squatting in mystical flames;
the third, a punky New Yorker, her hair a halo of spikes,
sculpting men becoming angels or the other way around;
the fourth, a Seattle printmaker who settled us all down
with talismans to ward off the demons we had brought with us;
and finally the fifth wheel—how would *they* describe *me*?
"the so-called writer working on her two-year writing block."

Those first few weeks were torture: all day I sat at the desk,
facing the blank wall like a child enduring her punishment;
then I moved the desk to the window for a front row view of Eden,
a garden path trailing down to the bowl of a Greek amphitheater.
Concert nights I could sit for free, listening on my balcony
to Julio Iglesias singing his Hispanic yuppie *boleros*.
In the mornings the bells announced daily mass at the piazza
in the chapel that contains the relics of Saint Stanislaus—
the pope's idea of a gift, the remains of a Polish saint.
Once I knelt at his niche and asked him to work his magic.

But nothing worked, not the printmaker's crowing rooster talisman;
not a cleansing by the German nor an angel from the punkster;
nor Mike arriving with dope and an amorous proposal;
none of it could roll back the big boulder of silence
and release the voice that would gather the scattered pieces together
and tell me at last the story of this life I had been living.
One morning—I'd had it!—clapping closed my blank notebook,
I went out on the balcony and caught sight of the little village.
—Boca, I later learned, at the mouth of the Chavón River.
Fishermen waist deep in water spread in a half circle,
their nets sieving the channel for the next meal for their children.
That's when I looked up and saw the movie-set village,

where I and the four elect were creating the culture of privilege,
the cobbled streets, the pretend church—something was missing!
Waving the guard *adiós*, I headed down the mountain.

II

Down that mountain, Mike and I hike
        calling out to each other,
"You all right, mate?"—like two Brits
        trekking through darkest Africa—
a movie scene we make up,
        confused as to how to behave.
We're not really the sunscreened tourists,
        pleasure colonists with charge cards;
not quite the Dominican rich
        phoning from our Mercedes
to alert the dozing watchman
        to get our weekend villa ready,
make sure the orchids are blooming,
        the beach sky producing sunshine.
Mike and I hike down that mountain
        stoned out of our minds,
on a joint he snuck in through customs
        I warned him not to bring.
Me, in my homeland fishbowl
        —pedigree Third World—
uncles in high places;
        religious childhood aunts swore
to save me during this visit,
        American lost-sheep niece,
all she needs is 20 pounds,
        un esposo, and of course, Jesus;
under which triple prescription

a skinny white man from Alabama,
Mike—with a joint in his pocket
            and a night kit full of rubbers—
nowhere fits the clean bill of health
            la familia had hoped to give me.
Mike and I hike down that mountain
            on a dirt path the servants use
that plunges into the bush
            as if into our worst fears.
Campesinos stop to stare
            at the blond-haired, blue-eyed marvel,
a *dominicana* in tow—
            "not choosing her own people . . .
of us and not with us"—
            whispering disapproval.
"You all right, mate?" Mike keeps calling
            as we thrash down to the river.
Across the choppy channel waters
            lies the little fishing village:
wooden hovels, thatched roofs,
            a fine residence at the tip.
I signal to that far shore,
            and the ferryman Papito
launches his leaky rowboat
            into the narrow channel
carrying us over strong currents
            to the waterbound peninsula
where another country waits,
            the one I came to discover.

III

Mike and I tour Boca, watched as we walk down Main Street,
a dirt path of tire tracks and traffic of skinny mongrels.
Across the river, we spot the towers of Altos Artist Colony,
an odd name for an art post on this post colonial island.
We've left that world behind, hiking down to this fishing village,
our possessions safely stowed in our luxury apartment.
Tonight we'll sleep well-cushioned on an orthopedic mattress,
thoughts muddled, hearts torn between comfort and compassion.
With them but not of them: the phrase runs through my head.
Giving our backs to Altos, Mike and I head down Main Street.

We walk past Leo's bodega, where a small audience has gathered
to watch our Hansel and Gretel cast adrift in the Third World,
surrounded by hungry children, vying with palm-ribbed mongrels,
for whatever crumbs we might drop to mark our way back to Altos.
We walk haunted, hand in hand, imagining witches everywhere.
"Is it the dope or is this wild?" Mike rolls his eyes at the gawkers
looking out from a shack, behind the well, by the fishnets,
whispers of *"el gringo y su gringa dominicana."*
Witches of conscience croon, *This is the way the world lives.*
"It's wild," I whisper to Mike. "You got any more dope with you?"

Past Nicanor's Disco—we glance inside at an old man dancing;
past a falling-down schoolhouse; a fort manned by idle *guardias;*
past an evangelical church, a zealous hot pink for Jesus;
past the deserted *gallera,* littered with trampled feathers.
Sundays, the place fills with men, tenderly grooming their roosters,
rum bottles in hand, their week's pay stuffed in their pockets,
men about to lose their week's pay betting on favorite *gallos.*
At home a woman waits, parceling out those wages:
this much for the baby's milk, this much for tonight's dinner . . .

Far off she hears the shouts and the frantic flap of feathers,
cries vaguely like the ones she's used to hearing in passion.

Babies, babies—we lose count—Everywhere babies crying!
At every woman's breast an infant, on her lap last year's newborn;
knee babies, toddlers, children—runny-nosed, naked, bawling.
Babies with amazing names gotten out of the Bristol Almanac.
(Each day lists saints born, virgins raped, apostles martyred.)
The copy at Leo's bodega is used to name the town's newborns.
Names we hear their mothers call as we walk down Boca's streets:
Montesino! Ludivina! Consagrado! Esperanza!
Babies eating dirt—Mike bends down to shake their fists loose,
head haloed in sandy hair, eyes the turquoise of the ocean:
a white apparition sent to instruct them on basic hygiene.
The babies burst into tears and scramble back to their mothers.

We wander towards the ocean, past the fancy Casa Blanca,
a two-story villa built by the *el* rich *americano*,
windows flashing flirtatiously, balcony railings gleaming:
truly, a sight for sore eyes after a village of eyesores.
We stand looking at it a while, already feeling less guilty
—at least our flat is on loan, our luck full of self-criticism.
Ten minutes in Boca and we've already heard the story
of the old gringo who free zones over in La Romana.
He lived alone for many years—everyone thought he was funny—
until one day he came home with a girl from a nearby village,
Milagros, bowing her head as she stepped out of the Rover,
too timid to put on airs, young enough to be his granddaughter.
She moved in—never comes out—people wonder what she's up to
since the gringo's gone all day, and they don't have any babies.
Sometimes the townspeople spot her passing by an open window,
calling down to the gardener or singing love songs with the radio.
Mike and I listen, intent on anyone else's love story.

We walk past the sailor's house, his pretty wife hides behind him;
past a thatched roof on four posts, the walls hauled off for kindling;
on the stone floor boys have spilled a soapy *higüero* of water;
they slide the length of the hut, calling out dares to each other.
House after house of palm wood, dried mud, concrete, cardboard,
until coming around full circle we're back at Leo's bodega
about to go in for beer and a shot of conversation.
When suddenly, out of nowhere, a crowd of children emerges,
Boca's babies, shedding their fears, sent by their mothers, begging.
They tug on Mike's pants, chorusing, "*¡Peso! ¡Peso! ¡Peso!*"
Mike dispenses his small change, but still they scamper behind him.
Wailing, the crowd grows, the children shove at each other.
"Jesus!" Mike rolls his eyes. "Is it the dope or is this wild?"
I, too, feel worn at the edges, but this, after all, is my homeland,
so taking Mike by the hand, Our Lady of Sudden Rescues,
I lead him down the cliff steps to the very tip of the island.

Where we watch the waves rolling in, the river flowing to meet them—
a parable we remark for letting ourselves be taken
by forces grander than just our personal satisfaction.
Coming down from our high, we kiss, tempted to making promises.
"I love you." Mike takes my hand, then waits for an echoing answer.
"*Te amo,*" I try in Spanish, since in English it sounds dishonest.

We climb up the rocky steps, having made our declarations.
Back on Main Street, wary, we look both ways for the children.
At last we can relax—they've been called home by their mothers:
Montesino! Ludivina! Consagrado! Esperanza!
Grand-sounding names that suggest history's selfless heroes—
men and women who died by the truths that they believed in.

I hadn't fit into any of the stories—that was the problem—
like Cinderella's ugly sister with a shoe store worth of discards—
not the love story, the sob story, the homegirl-made-good story.
That's why I came back to the island, why I headed down the mountain,
my only path I was making, one foot ahead of the other.
I'd bypassed the other stories afraid of their golden cages,
pretty heroines rattling the bars after their happy endings.
Worthy causes sounded the call—the best headed for the front lines—
but I hung back, unsure, if this was the thing I'd die for,
and so perhaps never found what it was I would live for.

So many years of hearing, "Go back to where you came from!"
of being *out* looking *in* created a certain cynicism—
this was *their* USA, *their* Vietnam, *their* racism,
their white girls in granny dresses talking about feminism,
the same white girls who years back in matched Villager outfits
taunted my sisters and me to the tune of "Chiquita Banana"—
Petty wrongs which self-doubt used as a fund of excuses
for not partaking of any of the holy human communions.
A pride of separateness led to a habit of seclusion
until even the friendly knock seemed an unwelcome intrusion.

A happy immigrant home might have offset the unwelcome:
the six of us marching abreast, arms hooked into each other's,
singing the USA anthem to the tune of a good merengue.
But as the plane lifted off from our motherland island,
the ground of *familia* gave, and the craziness started.
I felt a visceral yank at the center of my being,
as if an umbilical cord were being strained to the utmost—
all it needed was the jolt of my pen landing on paper

for the cord to snap off and leave me pathetically stranded
on the snowy blank page struggling with a new language.

I learned quick: inside a year I composed a poem in English,
directing my wary words through the wilds of strange vocabulary
to get to that intimate place I couldn't get to in person,
inside my reader's head as she read what I had written.
This was closer than friendship with none of the evasions,
closer at times than blood with its muddled entanglements,
outlasting passion, too, with its morning-after cautions.
I began writing in earnest—the city melted away,
the cruelty in the playground, the fierce struggles at home.
I had found the portable homeland where I wanted to belong.

No excuse—no matter how good—holds over the long run
for withholding yourself from your life, giving it all to paper.
For although as the saying goes in my Dominican Spanish,
el papel lo aguanta todo, the paper can hold anything,
it needs the breath of your breath, the bone of your living bone,
to become incarnate truth in the yearning heart of your reader.
So mid-life, finding my life aligned in the wrong direction,
I needed to find true north by the things that were important,
and remembering that first mother of my orphaned sensibilities,
I mounted a silver Pegasus and headed south to the island.
Yippee-oh! Yippee-oh! The plane soared over snowy farmlands.
Chiquita, I was on my way back to where I came from!

V

Mike and I pretend we're married, dodging questions why we're not,
New Age couple without rings—not so New Age here at all—
most couples can't afford rings, can't afford marriage, true love.
But for the gringo in the big house who has given his live-in maid

a thin band with a sparkly stone, engaging but not committed.
"He can have the milk for free, why bother buying the cow?"
The men elbow each other, strutting their male know-how.
Boca's men are as full of conquest as the first conquistadores,
who five hundred years ago stepped foot on this promontory.
The Tainos hid in caves that still line the Chavón River—
an old crone proposes this course to Boca's put-upon women.
The Tainos were smart men: they named the island Quisqueya,
The Mother of All the Earth, the female who made everything.
"You men," the crone concludes, "wouldn't be here without us!"
Boca's men pretend their hearts are overloaded with feeling,
but the truly burdened muscle is well below where they gesture.
They shamelessly talk the young girls into bedding down "forever,"
but by sun-up they are gone in their boats named after women.
So it goes, Boca's soap, the plot painfully predictable,
the men romancing the women for a taste of their El Doradoes,
proposing a church wedding at the first sign of a baby.
Those babies now bawling for milk, Those would-be husbands gone.
Men here generous of sperm, laying up two or three women,
spare on cash, spare on caretaking of children.
"Each child is born," they say, "with its loaf of bread under its arm."
Sometimes angry at their machismo, I give Mike one of my lectures,
or advise the wives to withhold, or the young ones not to marry.
But better a no-good man than none at all, the women argue.
Mike and I look at each other, his gaze is the first to falter.

VI

Boca's mayor calls Mike over to his one-room shanty office:
"You want I build you a house, take care of it while you're gone?
We want your kind around." He pinches Mike's pale arm
as if assessing the grade of merchandise he is buying.
Mike grins, T-shirted, sneakered, pony tail recently lopped off,

a concession to his visit to be introduced to my family.
The mayor dons his baseball cap, sporting a Playboy logo,
rabbit ears crest the head of this Nazi *dominicano*.
A little Adolf, Boca's mayor wants to lighten his constituency:
whiter skin, lankier hair, more American dollars.
"What do you say?" he asks Mike.
                              "What does he say?" Adolfo asks me.
—Adolfo, of course, not his name, but my revenge of a nickname—
"Nice house, a little garden, one, two, three, you're at the beach.
One, two, three," he looks at me,
                              "Tell your husband what I'm saying."
He nods eagerly concurring as I tell Mike, "He's trying to con you."

In his office cheap frames display official-looking documents:
his name in script attests to an auto mechanic diploma,
his hog came first at La Feria, he married María Paulina.
A distorted touched-up photo of the eighty-year-old president
hangs beside the pale trio of the fathers of our country:
Duarte, Sánchez, y Mella—whose desperado mustaches
make them look oddly like thugs in a low-budget gangster movie.
Our Lady of Altagracia, blue-eyed, blond under her veils,
tops the light-skinned assembly now gathered in Boca's town hall.

"Please," Adolfo invites us, arranging two chairs before him,
then takes his place at his desk, lacing his grease-stained fingers.
We sit in silence a moment, grinning foolishly at each other.
The desk is bare but for three important-looking black notebooks
stacked neatly before our host, each one of the town registers:
BIRTHS—MARRIAGES—DEATHS, the three official transactions.
Adolfo picks up the first book and reads us the latest entry:
Evangelista Altagracia, born a couple of weeks ago.
The next book, he solemnly opens, is heavy with Boca's losses.
Adolfo reads out the latest: Evangelista Altagracia,

her name penciled in just days after her birth was recorded.
The last book has no label and the fewest used-up pages,
Adolfo clears his throat and announces this year's one marriage:
Ana Morla wed Juan Mir after a half century together.
Couples in town can't afford the fifty pesos Adolfo quotes us
to be written into a book in a hog farmer's loping handwriting.
So they wait and save their money until one golden anniversary
they round up *la familia* for a pig-roast celebration,
Adolfo ceremoniously writing them in his black book.
I translate for Mike, who grins, shaking his head at the mayor,
who studies us a long moment, "You are married, señora?"
I shake my head, avert my eyes, as if ashamed to be discovered.
Adolfo's face softens with wiles. "Let me be the one to do it!"
He smiles a golden smile, twenty carats of phony friendliness.
"Just write your names down here without any obligation."
The mayor pats his chest, looks up, shrugging apologies:
he has nothing to write with. But like any would-be writer
—even a two-year block hasn't cured me of the habit—
I carry my favorite pen and my address-book-size journal.
Adolfo opens his book, and Mike signs our names with a flourish,
then leans over for a kiss as if we'd just gotten married.
Adolfo claps his congratulations, then pocketing my Bic,
he stacks up his three books, stops, smacks himself on the cheek.
We've signed out in his death notebook in unerasable ink!

VII

"We also die," says Ñaña, "we also hurt,"
pinching the honey-brown skin on her lean forearm,
wincing, until I reach over, prying her fingers open.
She has called me off the street, latched shut her door and window,
so the mayor won't overhear as she whispers her Magna Carta.
She crosses her hands at the wrists, rolling her eyes townward.

"That no good mayor, I tell you, governs only for himself.
A tourist who like you came not long ago on a visit
left him five hundred pesos to distribute among us poor;
he pocketed it and came by giving out free hellos!"
Ñaña straddles her crate stool, patting her empty pockets;
her hands constantly translate what she says into gestures.
(Perhaps she can reach deaf ears with this manual translation?)
Between talk, she stuffs the ends of her pigtails in her mouth
as if to stave off the hunger nibbling at her attention.
At her feet a toddler whines, light-eyed, a kinky blonde.
"I'm raising her for my daughter, who had to leave town to work.
Now the gringo's got his girl no one's hired at the big house.
I had nineteen, buried six, raised a handful for sickly women—"
she claps her hands on her breasts—
"but a woman runs out of goodness."
She has called me off the streets, thinking maybe I can help her,
with my good Spanish and sunglasses, surely I have connections?
"We need medicine," Ñaña says, "we need work and a road to get there!"
Through the back door falls a shaft of late afternoon sunshine
swarming with golden motes Ñaña's hands keep disturbing.
A sack of charcoal bricks lies covered in a dark corner,
a bread pudding dusted with flies sits on a wobbly table.
Ñaña's two means of livelihood could land her behind bars:
"It's illegal to burn trees and to sell *dulces* now requires
a license I can't afford. Tell me my hands aren't tied?"
Her hands close into fists, crossed at the wrists as if handcuffed,
a gesture sadly reminiscent of that childhood guessing game:
two fists, one with a prize, are held before you to choose;
you tap, the hand uncurls its treasure or disappointment.
But sometimes as a trick, both hands open insolvent,
bare as Ñaña's palms lined only with her bad fortune.

VIII

Clairol, the youngest of Ñaña's girls, has a two-year-old
and bad luck in jobs—Jack of all trades of the poorly paid:
she's been a factory worker, piecing together shirts and slacks;
a *niñera* for spoiled girls; cleaned a bishop's mistress' house;
made and sold sweets at stands in Boca and La Romana;
and once at La Caña Bar, she was picked up by a customer,
and back at his room in a bed big enough for a dozen kids,
she earned a month's wages doing less and enjoying more
than she'd ever done in a job before—the pity being
the two-year-old, her skin as pink as a conch shell lip,
who will never know who her father is
unless he returns to La Caña Bar with his daughter's face,
and the barman Juan tells the gringo how
Clairol's working now in the laundry
washing sheets for the bed she made she must now lie in.

Sheet after sheet she folds in the standard square,
putting away his sea-blue eyes and his golden hair—
whoever he is, whoever he was—
for the truth is with the dark night and the rum she drank
though watered down by the barman Juan,
she doesn't recall what the man looked like—
whoever he is, whoever he was.
She's made him up from her daughter's face
and the pretty men who all look like dolls
in the magazines that the tourists leave behind.
Sixteen years ago she herself was named
for a curly blonde in a shampoo ad
and her own Charmin was another find in a magazine.

In the humid heat of the laundry room Clairol's hair kinks up,
and her fingers swell so she can't take off the wedding band
she had to wear on her last job
for the foreman there would inspect more than the double seams
the girls bending over slacks—and away from him—reinforced.
Clairol irons out the worry lines on a pillowcase;
the calm smell of the warm cloth soothes her weary heart.
Towering stacks of towels and sheets depart each day
and come back at night in a soiled pile from the very bed
where three years ago in a haze of rum and *novela* dreams
Clairol lost her head and awoke in this pretty mess she's in.
She knows now she mistook her role on those t.v. soaps
for the lucky girl waiting for his knock.
Now she knows who she really is, who she really was:
the buffoon maid opening the door to the handsome man.
A good job, not a fantasy, is all she wants.
And the pay is bad and her hands are chapped from detergent soaps,
but Clairol likes the clean control of this latest job.
And she prays bad luck won't strike again, and she'll find herself
without honest work at La Caña Bar having to pick up
the next meal and the next child she doesn't want.

IX

El profesor Juan Bautista is teaching the two times table
to fourteen of Boca's kids ranging in age from five to fifteen.
Near the back door the whiz kid in the end pew to himself
is doing the seven times table—or should be, at any rate.
On the sly he's sketching a boy looking in at a store window.
The little schoolhouse is closed, no money to do repairs,
so *el profesor* holds class in the church before the altar
under the watchful eyes of Jesus about to expire
but not yet fully graduated from the flesh into the spirit.

El profesor is a hothead who keeps cool before the authorities.
After all, as a *chavonero*, he can put two and two together.
The front doors have been latched as if class were a secret meeting
for the two times table, he knows, can be inflammatory business.

El profesor goes down the rows, quizzing each of his charges.
"Two times zero is how much?" He points with a little switch
known for doing double service.
                              "Two times zero," the chosen one stands,
"is the main dish of the poor man!"
                              "Good!" The professor nods,
"Now finish the rest of the table."
                              "Two times one is me by myself
looking for my advantage. Say, I've eaten my piece of *pan*,
I snatch my brother's from his hand, feed my hunger twice over.
Two times three is me with my friends,
smaller shares, but more satisfaction.
And two times four is how much we laugh,
and times five the fun when we share it.
Times six, times seven, the days pass;
two times eight years, I'm a man,
but my life is on display with my brothers' at a shop window,
two times nine pesos is written on a little hidden price tag,
and chances are two times ten, I'll ever afford to buy it."

"Good!" *El profesor* grins, his switch transforms into a wand,
waving blessings on the star, then signals to the next student.
"Three times zero is how much?" Each pupil recites his litany,
until the professor arrives at the whiz kid near the back door
in an ironed shirt that shows he's being lovingly looked after,
sent to school without fail, fed his bread with a wipe of butter.
That's why he's up to his sevens and knows numbers past a thousand.

El profesor points to the back door to be opened a crack for air,
then nods to the secret artist to begin his recitation.

"Seven times zero," the boy stands, "is no money in my pocket.
Times one is a week of daydreams about what I'd buy for my family
if I had seven times three pesos in my two pockets!
Seven times four," the boy continues without any hesitation . . .
A breeze blows in off the sea, *seven times five*, it whispers;
times six, times seven, the waves break on Boca's rocky shoreline.
How many times can we multiply hopes and come up with nothing?
Seven times eight sets of bones lie in the graveyard for asking.
The priest preaches *paciencia* to *los pobres chavoneros*,
"Your rewards will come hereafter, multiplied one hundredfold."
But the bright kid in his clean shirt nearing seven times two years old
wants his hundredfold now—food for his sisters and brothers.
"Seven times nine," he's reciting, as a breeze blows in the back door,
lifts his paper off his pew, up over his head it hovers,
then slowly descends like a message from the pen of the Almighty.

El profesor looks down at his feet, his switch imminent with punishment,
but he smiles when he sees the work of the seven times table artist.
A storefront of little faces all duplicates of his pupils
are tagged with high price numbers tied at each neck like nooses.
They peer out at the consumer—while behind this odd display—
a likeness of the professor has put aside his habitual switch
and snips with a pair of scissors seven times two kids free!

                            X

The shy schoolgirl in pigtails bends over her notebook,
her head filling with the word she's spelling,
as if by the abracadabra of the alphabet

125

she could summon up
a world better than the one she lives in.

C.A.M.A.
She sleeps on a soft mattress.
V.E.S.T.I.D.O.
Her shift turns into a petticoat
covered by a rose-red party dress.

The girl bends to her work,
her body twisting as she copies out
in tortured script the tidy alphabet
her teacher writes out
on the model top line.

Capitals and lowercase line up to spell the world:
Big *A*, hands on her hips,
strides over distances
while little *a* tags behind,
wagging her puppy tail;

big *B* puffs out his bully chest
while little *b* proudly imitates;
big *C* smiles at her perfect child,
a small nostalgic version of herself;
little *d* mirrors big *D*'s Roman belly.

All the way through the alphabet
as if through a human family,
the lowercase alters
but cannot escape
the precedent of its capital.

All of this insight is dawning in the schoolgirl.
All of this light is breaking in her dark brown eyes.
All she can do is hope not to copy out
the sad example of her mother's life
she does not want.

Now in the blazing sun of her noonday dreams,
the girl walks home, numbers swirling
like dust motes in her head:
How many sisters, brothers, mouths to feed?
How many names to learn to spell?

Her mother's many worries
she can't count to yet.
And then, how light and sweet,
to say the simple charm
of her own name, *Luz*,

light skipping its sunbeams in her path,
making the tin roofs gleam
like a jeweler's shop;
Luz spelling today's new word,
a letter a step—

C.A.S.A.
a yellow house with a tile roof . . .
on an emerald lawn with a turquoise pool . . .
in a pretty town where a schoolgirl walks
taking little steps so as not to spill

this splendid world that the words construct
as she rounds the corner towards the two-room shack
without windows, paint, or a finished roof

—coming into view . . .
just waiting for Luz to say the magic word.

XI

The little house is closed up—faded turquoise with salmon trim,
wooden boards and a tin roof, middle-class house in Boca.
Mike and I stop several times, exclaiming it sure looks cute.
A passing-by neighbor shrugs when we ask if anyone lives there—
a local gesture which translates, *I don't know which truth to tell you.*
I answer back with a smile, *Tell me the happy version!*
We look at the locked door as if waiting for it to open.

"A year ago a gringa moved here—nobody knew who sent her—
she wasn't one of the peace kids or the sunburnt missionaries,
nervous, bony, past first bloom, suddenly here among us.
We didn't know what to think, rumors spread she was spying.
The mayor checked on her daily, reported she was unhappy.

"Twice a day she walked through town to buy food at Leo's bodega:
three plantains, a couple of eggs, a wedge of cheese if there was any—
certainly not enough to keep body and soul together.
We pitied her, kept a hello warm for her coming and going.
Our friendliness did the trick: she hired a local woman
to cook her something substantial and sun her bedding on the bushes.
The gringa, Morena told, used a little book for talking
but said nothing to explain the slow change coming upon her.
Week by week the gringa filled out and soon there was no question—
though Morena swore no man (but the mayor) had been to visit.
The gringa seemed not to know she was carrying a little future.
Mornings, evenings, she waddled by, no mention of preparations.
Morena said inside the house it was like no baby was coming,
no cradle, no little clothes, no rags put by for the birthing.

Maybe this was to be another Immaculate Conception
—except this time the surprise was being sprung also on Mary!
As we always do, we women provided for what was missing—
Primitiva whose hand has spanked air into most of our bodies
was on call for when the gringa began her terrible moaning—
there needs no little book to translate a child's coming.

"A few weeks short of nine months like an unwitting Joseph,
Morena's son shows up at the end of the cane harvest.
The gringa—on a whim—moved him in, and who could gossip?
What was the man to cook with the oven already occupied?
One morning Morena came and found the little house vacant,
on the table in dollar bills were the wages she had coming,
and a paper sack addressed *To the Mayor of Boca*
with *the money I owe you*, and a note asking his pardon.

"Most weekends Bruno visits with the gringa and her baby,
everyone saying how much that pale boy looks like his father,
smiling and looking at Bruno, a big slow dreamy black man,
who acts as if he conceived that child *en ausencia*.
Bruno's still with the gringa, we can't figure out what she's after.
But why pull a plant from the soil to see if the roots have sprouted?
They get on well...never argue...never talk much for that matter,
for all Bruno learned in school was to daydream out the window,
and a *please, you're welcome, thank you* for talking to *los turistas*.
So what can the two exchange except the babble of Babel
and the fluency of flesh that needs no further translation."

Mike and I stand at the gate while I translate the gringa's story.
His hand on my shoulder droops an epaulette of long fingers,
freckled and pink with sun next to my deepening olive.
"Not bad timing," he observes, "old Bruno wasn't a dummy!
He shows up and rescues the girl at the end of a sad love story.

He got all the forward force of the love she'd been expecting,
and in addition the gratitude of saving her heart from breaking."
That's one way to think of the story is what I find myself thinking
as I translate myself inside the shuttered house and imagine
looking out at a foreign world that doesn't promise to love us
but leaves us without just cause alone to our own devices.
"Not bad timing," I agree, "that old gringa wasn't a dummy!"
Our laughter rings as we walk up to the door to meet them—
maybe we'll catch them home on one of their weekend visits,
this eleventh hour couple who have set our own clocks ticking.
We want to hear for ourselves the conclusion of their story
as if with that *all's clear*, we'll begin our own adventure.
Fists posed to knock—we freeze. Are *we* ready for happiness?

XII

"Tell me," I ask Miguel Angel, picking up each of his *santos*,
"which one to buy? Which one will draw song to paper?
Which one will flood my heart again with passion for a man?
Which one will help me make up
my divided Dominican-American mind?"

At his makeshift street booth under whose counter top he sleeps,
the black man smiles, all gums, but for a few luminous teeth,
a Haitian *houngan*, brought over to work the sugar cane fields.
He stayed, paying through his back then full set of teeth
for the forged Dominican I.D. he flashes at me, soiled, dog-eared,
so that the Miguel Angel in the small, over-exposed Polaroid
seems one of the little *santos* I've been leafing through,
who could cure heartache, help me win the National Lottery.
"You see?" Miguel Angel asks. I nod as if I knew
what revelation he intended with his forged credentials,
pulling up so close I can smell his cure-all body odor,

which could decongest blocked passages, make the blind blink,
an odor to enhance a *houngan*'s reputation, zombie rich.

Already bewitched, I do not draw away
but disclose my woes in detail to this stranger:
my inability to fall in love with the right men,
my two-year writing block, reclusiveness, my fear of moving
so that I'll likelier live in exile than risk the passage home.
On and on, enumerating, eyes closed the better to focus in
on the obsessive core—as if this street corner faith healer,
whose hands I feel now cap my shoulders,
could lift me from that middle-aged self,
empty of passion, empty of song,
a heart so cracked it sieves even the strongest feelings.

But when the wave of yearning passes, opening my eyes,
I find the *houngan* peering down my jersey sundress,
his gaze so unabashed I assume lust, too, is part of his healing,
as he commences chanting, his feet stamping,
body swaying, hands vibrating spirit power into my body,
as he cries out in Boca's dead-end street,
the names of his riders:

> *¡Santa Clara! ¡Metrecelí!*
> *¡Doctor Gregorio Hernández!*
> *¡San Juan de la Conquista,*
> *por la virtud que tú tienes*
> *repártele el compañero*
> *que a ella más le conviene!*

On and on, his erection hard against my right thigh,
as if this were the spur of his spirits, riding him further,
further into the flesh they long for, bodiless.

> *Móntese, doña, móntese,*

I hear the *houngan* cry.
Climb on!

I give a little hop, self-conscious now that we've come apart,
he, the *houngan*; I, the overgrown skipping-rope girl
with a bandaged scraped knee,
making a wish on first stars in the sky,
waiting to have my turn on the carousel ride.
And now, at last, the good life's ready for me
like a brushed-down stallion,
a saddle strapped on his chestnut back,
his neck bowing, feet stamping
as I take the reins into my trembling hands.

XIII

At his bodega, Leo sells everything from nail polish to dried leaves:
leaves for brewing potent teas, leaves to help you get your man back,
leaves to get you with child, leaves to flush out a child
the wrong father put inside you—Leo winks pointing to those leaves,
his hands scratching at his crotch, an unsettling tic of his.
You glance away at his nail polish . . .

If you see it, it's for sale inside Leo's bodega:
a glass case of crumbling *dulces*, a humming freezer of Presidentes,
sacks of rice and beans, rows of cans, solutions for kinky curls,
whitening creams for the sweet, honey-skinned Boca girls.
In a back room Leo runs *una barra restaurante*,
more *barra* than *restaurante* according to Boca's mothers!
The front doors open wide on a sweeping view of the river
emptying into the bay, sea breezes stirring the *palmas*.
Even at noon it's cool enough inside Leo's bodega
to keep his hot temper warm, his *queso de crema* from melting.

While you wait, order a beer and a ten cent shake from the nut jar.
Why not a lucky *billete* with whatever change you had coming?

Leo's got selling in his blood if his weren't sealed in his veins
he'd sell you a pint or two, use the profit to buy a tonic
to make his body produce stronger and better inventory.
He's got a touch of the Grand Seigneur
with his bare chest and Virgen's medallion,
his kinky hair a prestigious white, his eyes full of boyish mischief;
he'd welcome the thought of his blood coursing through all of Boca,
especially in the sweet-scented breasts of *las señoritas*.
Leo laughs, clapping his hand just below his shaking belly
as if containing his laughter at the root of its hilarity.

Although everything's for sale: one thing Leo gives out free,
especially to women, and especially to one type—
he can spot her when she comes in: dark bags under her eyes,
her skin hanging on her bones like a soaked dress left to dry,
her eyes vacant as if you'd snapped a locket open and gazed
at nothing but a glassy oval instead of a sweetheart's face.
That's the type Leo tries to engage in conversation,
giving her free *menticas* or a sample of *dulce de leche*,
and should anyone accuse him of being a soft touch,
he sneers, he wants her alive long enough to make a purchase!

"Advice is free," he'll tell her once he's drawn her into talking.
"You tell me what's going wrong. I'll tell you how to correct it."
In most cases it's some brand of male disappointment—
another-woman, not-in-love, too-attached-to-his-mother.
There are many ways for a man to cause a poor woman heartache,
but only one foolproof cure: dump him, find another,
and when he begins to cause you more heartache than flutter,

drop him, find another, the point is to keep moving,
until one day, skinny and sad, you enter Leo's bodega,
and he pokes his pocket knife at you with a wedge of *dulce de leche*,
his hands roost back at his crotch, fumbling with his endowment.

Once or twice, Leo admits, he's been at his wit's end—
a woman will come in beyond the reach of his salvation,
a woman so tied in knots his head throbs hearing her talking,
a woman who thinks too much, a woman who won't be mended,
a woman whose infinite longings aren't satisfied by the human.
"Too big an appetite of the spirit can starve the flesh into madness,"
Leo's face cracks with lines. He mends his scowl with a smile,
His hands rise from his crotch and bang down on the counter.
Ay, he hates the thought of a woman beyond the reach of his rescue,
but he lets her go for he knows if he can't save her, no one else can—
his is the only bodega in this little land's end village.
Sadly, he watches the waif walk out of his store, empty-handed,
his own hands fall limp at his sides, then plunge deep into his pockets.

XIV

Mike and I have our best talks sitting in Nicanor's disco,
the town's open air *barra*, a concrete floor, a thatched roof,
posts hung with paper lanterns and a poster of Madonna.
Her abundant breasts brim over a low-cut fishnet corset.
"What a catch!" the fishermen say, wiping their sweaty foreheads.
Every day of Mike's visit after our walk through Boca,
we stop to discuss the future, sipping warm Presidentes,
hoping to God Nicanor won't be sent for to oblige us
with pirated tapes played on his Japanese ghetto blaster.
I can't get no satisfaction, Nicanor mouths the lyrics,
clueless to what he's singing, *though I try, though I try*.

We've talked love as Plato's halves searching madly for each other,
but agree our mismatched selves don't exactly fit the model;
the Rilkean solitudes bordering and saluting each other
fit my nature just fine but strike Mike like a prison sentence:
"I'd sooner be racked over coals than have a Rilkean romance.
How about the Odysseyan model?" Mike's grin has a naughty tilt,
"I roam and you stay home fulfilling your Rilkean nature!"
We've discarded other versions: commuting couples, companions,
comrades in arms, open marriage, mutual muse and mentor—
none of which describe our rather recent relations,
a late night party air with day just about dawning.

Today, Mike insists it's time I introduce him to my family.
Hasn't he passed the litmus of visiting my homeland
with a low-key, non-tourist, non North American attitude?
(That cool attitude I suspect is more weed than strength of character.)
From her outpost Madonna puckers her breasts in our direction.
"Give a nice guy a break! Besides we're as good as married."
(Boca's mayor had us rewrite ourselves in his book of marriage.)
"I'm not 100% sure, but, hey, what's the worst that can happen?"
Mike laughs, clinking my glass, toasting the taking of chances,
a clink that will soon grow to a gong of alarm in my family.
Down Main the desperate strains of "Satisfaction" approaching . . .

XV

Our brief trip to the capital to surprise the family,
Mike and I had a bad fight on the shoulder off the highway;
the sea, pounding away at the rocks, sent up
a salty, spermy spray as if it were egging us on.
Several cars racing by slowed and honked
at this wildly gesticulating couple screaming *como dos demonios*
to be heard above the commotion of an emotional ocean,

above the sea breezes stirring the *palmas*,
the roar of Third World traffic with its falling-apart cars.
What was it we were yelling we could not bear
to hear the other one saying?

We headed off in separate directions, red-faced, on foot,
the rental car—on Mike's card—abandoned on the shoulder.
I couldn't help but admire his anger even in the midst of mine,
for I would have taken precautions, locked the doors,
rolled up the windows against those sudden tropical storms,
had the obligation been mine—which it also was,
50/50 couple that we were—but which I ignored—
part of my argument (now coming back to me) being precisely that:
I had always to be the grownup while Mike gallivanted around,
knowing he could always fall back on the net of my bottom line.
His argument? Hell, I couldn't hear what *he* was yelling about!

Mike stomped towards the capital; I was headed back to Boca
until a sense of the ridiculous made us both burst out laughing.
We each had a four-hour hike in our separate directions
and a big tab from BUDGET to pay should the Escort be vandalized.
We stopped, headed back, still giddy with temper,
but face to face, something gave, and we both began crying.
It was exhausting to fall in love in the middle of our lives,
all that adolescent angst coupled with mid-life crisis.
The minute we hit the capital we stopped at the first hotel,
a little seedy to be sure no family would be there,
then climbed in the lumpy bed and fell into a dead sleep.

But woke up mid night in a sweat holding on to each other.
Already we understood there would be no family meeting
as we lay in bed sadly listening to the traffic out the window.
"Tell me something you haven't told anyone,"

we asked as a pledge of allegiance,
secrets we would have sealed had we not been interrupted:
a drunk hunting for the john stumbled in in a shaft of light.
"Jesus, Mike, don't you lock doors?!" Another fight began brewing.
Next day in the lobby lounge the intruder kept eyeing me
until I was almost convinced he was somebody in the family.
But Mike translated the look: *I want to have my turn, too.*

The long ride back we talked openly of "the end of our relationship,"
where we were each headed the other wouldn't be going.
As soon as Mike graduated from his change-of-life nursing program,
he was off to the Third World—"to do goodness knows what good!
I'm old enough to know better"—his ideals tempered by cynicism:
a good combination, I thought, for anyone on a mission.
And I was back to the States if my wild vacillations
didn't land me in Boca like the gringa with her Bruno.
"Who knows?" I said when Mike kept asking what I was after.
"I have immortal longings in me," I quoted some famous writer.
But passing the scene of our fight, all I longed for was happiness.

XVI

"Who you love? Who you love?" she pesters
like a child, following behind us
with her jump-rope jingle minus the jump rope,
a young pretty woman flirting with Mike,
who's leaving, crossing back to the Altos side,
heading home the way Americans say *home*,
"last place I had a job or fell in love"—
a place she sees as Eden to this town
and this her only chance of getting out.
Abashed, I stand back, translator-on-call,
though instantly, Mike understands

what the young girl wants and grins . . .
the world already looking better, much better,
her dark curls swirling down her back,
her bright eyes hopeful for a better life.
And at the pit of my stomach I feel it
uncoiling its slick length, fanged and venomous,
the dark side of a love already spent—
(How dare she romance him until I'm done!)
Dismissing her, I see how privilege hums
down all the avenues of who I am,
how even what I loved *belongs* to me.

XVII

The old man sleeps like the dead under the thatched *bohío*,
beside fishermen mending their nets, done with the day's fishing.
The setting sun blurs the line where the burning sky becomes
the matching gold of the sea, earth and sky are now meeting.
The fishermen cross themselves—at certain times of the day,
God takes the world back—their hands working the knots
look to the eyes of faith like cherubim playing their harps.

Sometimes a jet roars by disrupting their evening angelus—
the fishermen shake their heads at this blasphemous intrusion.
"God gave us earth enough. We have no business up there!"
They motion, but the gold sky is one with the golden ocean.
"But you're fishermen," I point out, "you trespass daily on the sea,
the stormy sea shooing you out, the rough seas pounding your *yolas*,
the high sea putting up walls, miraculously you sail over them."

The fishermen nod their heads. "We follow His example.
He took His apostles to sea, walked on water to convince them.
On His own two feet He walked, not on planks yanked by a speedboat.

But He drew the edge of our world very clearly at the horizon.
You never hear of Him taking His crew of apostles to heaven—
though the open sky teems with stars and clouds of silvery mackerel
and provides a masthead view of His human congregation."

As we talk the bundle of rags uncurls a human being,
releasing a savage smell of not having washed in ages.
An old man in beggar's rags with a sensitive thinker's profile,
chocolate skin and a white beard, eyes luminous with intelligence,
sits up hugging one knee, eyes narrowed as if he were searching
for that fine line where the sky meets the twin-blue Caribbean.
Then to no one in particular he delivers his observation.

"A life lived as far as it goes is the only kind worth having."
He falls silent, I make up a tragic story to explain him:
Maybe his great love died or she left him for another
or he went mad . . . or . . . the mind scrambles to contain him
so that even the tragic stays penned in our understanding.
The fishermen all make signs, turning handwheels at their temples.
The oldest, most respected, gives me the beggar's biography.

"One day he walked into town—no one knew where he came from.
He wouldn't tell us his name, wouldn't say how he got here.
We fishermen fed him scraps, let him stay in our *bohío*;
then Leo, one day yakking, engaged him in conversation
and realized *el viejo* was book-learned with an elegant way of talking.
But just as suddenly as he'd snap out, he'd fall back into his trances,
and no one, not even Leo, could reach him in his crazed wandering.

"We took him in, our brother in Christ, welcomed him at our table
to feast on our day's catch and the milk of our human kindness.
Leo says he's from Baní and once gave his name as Fausto."

Fausto starts when he hears his name, peers out at the sea and sky,
his lips part in a cracked tooth smile, he shouts at the far horizon,
"Here I am!" The fishermen sigh, "He's calling out to his people."
But Fausto's glance is directed high above his human family.

"I give up, hide-and-seek Lord? I've been looking for a lifetime,
stretched my mind as far as it goes to the tip of my understanding.
Are you playing children's games with the toys of your creation,
sporting with our confusion, baiting us with half answers?
I want more of an explanation than is given in the Bible.
A new-born faith can live on bread, a sip of wine, a weekly homily,
but an aging soul requires a hardier diet of answers."

Fausto stops, scours the sky, as if he'd just heard a bee buzzing—
a tiny silver cross jets over the sky's calm ocean.
Fausto points to the thin white line that trails behind the aircraft
as if he would smudge it out and write down his own message
or keep the expanse blank for the scribbling of a seagull.
His hand megaphones at his mouth as he calls to the vanishing jet,
"Come down, fisher of men, see if you can catch us again!"

XVIII

One of *los muchos*, a boy about five,
                    tags behind me—
rolling a tire, piloting it with a stick,
                    rolling it so close
I'm afraid he'll run me over,
                    down the dirt path
to the rocky point, famous for sunsets,
                    today's minutes away—
a moment I want for myself.
                    But the boy dogs me,

rolling his dark zero
          up the rocky coast,
over the bad terrain,
          the tire wobbling wildly,
I dissuading him,
          "Won't your mother be worried?"
"You'll get a flat, you know?"
          dismissing him
with stronger and stronger words,
          as he pursues,
a tiny demon set loose to ask me
          one thing only,
"Un peso, un peso, un peso,"
          repeated over and over
without change in inflection
          as he rolls his tire
to where I sit under a grape tree,
          our Lady of Sunglasses
with the big black purse bag
          watching the sun slip
like a gold coin into the ocean's pocket.
          "Un peso, un peso, un peso"—
no coaxing, no sob story,
          the need obvious,
his sugar-sack shift peeled
          over a skinny shoulder,
his nose running.

          I peel off my glasses,
look him in the eye.
          "Give me peace," I say
in a voice as plaintive as his,
          "Peace, please."

He stops, the needle lifting
          from its groove
as he goes back over his few years,
          recollecting
if this has ever happened before?
          The tables turned—
the *patrona* begging him back!
          "Give me," he begins,
"Give me your glasses."
          "Give me peace," I reply.
"Give me your big black purse bag."
          "Peace," I whisper.
"Your sneakers," he begs, "give me your watch."
          "Peace, please,"
sounding less like a plea than a blessing,
          as I walk off
and he follows, inventorying
          all I'm carrying—
notebook, pen, water bottle—
          I wondering to what lengths
he'll take our strange interchange,
          if he'll beg
for my hair, teeth, flesh, bones
          when he's done
with my key chain and sweat socks?

          We walk the rocky inlet,
he pleading, *"Déme un peso."*
          I pleading,
"Give me peace, please!"
          Until we both fall silent,
exhausted by crying out
          our unheeded needs.

And the only sounds now
        are the thumps of his tire
and his footsteps dogging mine,
        to land's end and back
he pursues me, implacable,
        accusing with his silence,
wanting, finding me wanting.

XIX

I've met everyone in Boca as if I'm running for office,
but still I can't find the place where I come into their story,
settle down in a tinker-toy shack, become the first lady of Boca,
in other words just another goddamn character in their story,
which bothers me—I admit it!—ceding control of the narrative.
"She came here with her gringo, holding hands like scared children,
smoking the giggly weed in the rocks by Don Charlie's villa.
They visit a couple of weeks, then the weakling couple split,
the man like a smart man happened upon the wrong thing takes wing;
she stay—Lord can tell what she want! walking around,
writing things down in that little tablet like she making us up!"

Here's the story I left behind in the USA I deserted—
left my job, friends, apartment—I couldn't hold it together,
the American dream narrative I was experiencing as a nightmare.
A few days before I ran off from that weary midwestern city,
I had back-to-back appointments at the Total Health Care Facility:
psychiatrist, ophthalmologist, both visions were failing me.
I was given my medical records to walk to the nurse's station.
Ay, but that thick envelope was burning a hole in my fingers.
I detoured into the bathroom, in a stall tore the seal open,
then read with voracious eyes the nearly illegible jottings:
"Panicked Hispanic Female afflicted with magical thinking."

There was, of course, more I'd blabbed to that stern Illinois doctor
on the off chance he'd have, as I told him, "string for the labyrinth."
His impassive face showed only a quivering of the eyebrows.
Really, what could that white boy afflicted with a cruel crewcut
(I could see the pink scalp and the swathes of the barber's razor)
prescribe for a panicked Hispanic heartsick in the heartland?
There in the bathroom stall facing my odd reflection,
an elongated El Greco face in the toilet roll dispenser,
I laughed till I peed, charmed by this lovely diagnosis.
Yes, like the poet said, words could stay the confusion:
I could live with magical thinking. I flushed in celebration!

Two stories, one in the past, the other I was composing
one foot ahead of the other, the way that our lives get written
on the path that's only seen with the hindsight of arrival . . .
And already I was detouring from the plot I'd set in motion
by settling down in a village where I had no business living.
I was a foreigner in Boca from a country even further
than the USA they could get to with a green card or on a *yola*;
I came from the monied class—and although I rejected the label,
I knew in the back of my mind, there were safety nets below me:
in a pinch if I said the word, hands would be there to catch me,
the chauffeured Mercedes would come and cart me off to the capital.

But the greatest net of all was the one I made with language,
the precarious world underlaid by the sturdy net of a narrative.
Silence had been the closest I had come to true impoverishment.
But although to my ravenous spirit it seemed a terminal hunger,
and Williams claims men can die for lack of the literary,
words are a second course to the famished of the Third World.
Surrounded by Boca's starving I was shamed into action:
fund raising, office trotting, in a month's time we were promised

a schoolhouse, a dispensary, a better road than the channel crossing.
Now I wanted the reward built into this kind of a narrative:
a happy ending to close at least one version of my story.

XX

My last afternoon in Boca, Luisa crooks her finger
behind her husband's back, and I follow her
to a locked hut at the back of their rubble yard.
Inside, a dozen votive candles flicker
before a wall of *santos*, each with a service
laid out on the table, knives in water,
crossed candles, a cigar and a glass of rum,
egg shapes stewing in jars of cloudy water.
Dumbfounded, I ask, "Why behind Leo's back?"
And as she binds her head in the yellow kerchief
and hands over the red for me to put on,
she rolls her eyes and says, "You know
how the men get nervous when we women talk."
I feel nervous, too, for her voice is deepening
with the weight of her spirit rider on her back,
her neck twisting this way and that as she speaks.
"You are going to a strange land over water,"
the heavy voice says, "prepare to lose your way.
For those born to a *santo* must stay put
to ground that power in the land it loves.
It's a wonder you haven't gone mad reining it in."
As she talks, she tightens the kerchief on my head
like a tourniquet, so I feel my temples pulse
as if a *santo* were confirming her diagnosis.
"Used to be a time," I find myself explaining,
my voice growing heavy with acknowledgment,
"a time I might have come back here to live:

everything in me tentative and toying
with loyalties, a young girl up for grabs.
Those were the times a man seemed enough roots,
the bed of love seemed the homeland that I wanted.
But after several heart-breaking transplantings,
I needed a steadier source of nourishment,
something to plant at the center of my life,
something that would require all of me
and which by laboring at I might become
someone I couldn't take back: my own woman.
Ay, Luisa, it's hard to explain in my childhood Spanish,
but you know how you've chosen to practice *santería*—"
"Chosen?" she interrupts, the yellow bulb
of her kerchiefed head like a lighted-up idea—
"You think this is choice?" She points to the wall
studded with *santos*: Lucía proffering eyeballs;
Gregorio posing as a country doctor;
draped in her jewels, the coquette Metrecelí.
"Does the bird need to remind itself, Sing!
Or the sea, Wave! Or the wind, Blow!
No—" she shakes her head in reply—
"The *santos* choose us, all we do is comply."
Angry at my irreverence, she unties
her kerchief, dusts off cobwebs
from the Hand of God, her trance
seemingly broken as she grumbles, "Choice!"
Truth is I don't know my own mind,
cooped up in her *santos* coop,
between the Scylla and the Charybdis
of two cultures, trying to explain myself
in the mother tongue I was weaned from as a child.
And so, begging the *santos*' and her pardon,
I agree, "Choice is a bad choice of words."

Her stifled smile shows she understands
the *santería* of the words I've chosen
to serve in another tongue, another country.
We eye each other shyly like new friends,
unsure after their first bad argument
if the friendship holds. Then, like the last rumble
of thunder after a storm, she grumbles, "Choice!
Don't be misled by choice away from your nature.
Life is more simple than you think. Come home
to serve your *santo* and your own people.
If you want a little more—" she cocks her head
beyond the latched door towards her husband's store—
"with the help of Metrecelí—" she winks—
"there's always a lot more of a little more."
And now in earnest she begins my education
this last afternoon in Boca, a crash course
on long distance easing of my *santo*'s need
until the day I can come back to live.
But even as I scribble down what she says,
I know I won't be following her prescriptions,
for where in the States will I find *el bini-bini*
or *la flor de la libertad, suerda con suerda?*
But it goes further than that: I know
I won't be coming back to live
in my ex-homeland. A border has closed like a choice
I can't take back. And the trouble isn't the new
but the shadow falling across it of the old,
every word alloyed by a Spanish version,
every choice daunted by a broken custom
as if I were seeing double, the life
I might have lived haunts the one I bungle
without self-confidence or precedence.
But Luisa blames my self-doubt on my *santo*,

doublecrossing my life with its homesickness.
This last afternoon in Boca at her altar,
shadows falling across it through the window
of palm trees swaying in nostalgic breezes,
I almost succumb to her simpler version,
closing my eyes, forgetting myself . . .
I feel her touch my forehead with her thumbs,
making a sign of the cross; I feel her breath
warm with my mother tongue offering me
the opportunity to meet my *santo*;
I feel her hands clamp down upon my shoulders
as if to fix me firmly in this soil.
Her feet are stomping welcome to my rider,
her body swaying to the beat they keep.
She almost lures me back with *santería*—
but just this moment Leo growing nervous
at her extended absence hurries back
through the rubble yard to see what is going on.
We hear him pausing at the door to listen,
then ordering her home, he breaks my trance.

XXI

I hear Papito calling that it's time,
now is the last crossing before dawn
when his ferryboat La Linda will fill up with regulars
on the first shift at Don Charlie's *factoría*,
and come back from the other side
with night watchmen returning from the villas,
easily triggered into angry talk
of how *los ricos* live like movie stars
while Boca's children die like matches, lit a minute,
¡Ay! and out they go. *Ay sí, señor.*

I hurry, anxious I'll be left behind,
through packed-earth streets, past Nicanor's disco
where in the ghostly gas lamp
brown-skinned beauties dance with their loose-limbed *novios*
to a static-ridden, battery-driven ghetto blaster;
past Ñaña's hovel, dark but for the flicker
between the palm leaves of illegal fires;
past Miguel Angel's street corner pantheon of *santos*,
each one laid out on the makeshift altar
with her *velita* and her dish of scented water,
and for one disembodied sweet-tooth
a spoon with a sticky wad of Leo's famous *dulce de leche;*
el profesor's new schoolhouse sleeps,
its freshly painted shutters shut, the mural barely visible
where each of his charges has drawn a life-size self
and signed his name.
One half-drawn figure I cannot make out,
unfinished, outlined in white paint, too white,
a ghost who came and left
in search of a happier ending
than what Boca affords,
a life of choice, a life of words.

Past Fausto looking up, night watching stars from his *bohío*,
I find the shore by following the lapping sound of water,
where Papito waits in his leaky rowboat,
the little town behind us going dark
but for the few trembling orbs of gas lamps,
the faint, transparent beams of worn-out flashlights.
And La Linda sinks a little with my coming on,
Papito launching her into the choppy channel, scrambling in
and crouching at his oars at the last minute.

I turn for a Lot's-wife last look—
and there, on the rocks beside the gringo's villa,
I can almost make her out, posed like a siren
on the barnacle-crusted cliffside, a white outline,
calling me to come back come back
from the self I toil over in the States . . .
as we move out deeper, the *vivero* filling,
the waves rocking La leaky Linda,
the disco's tinny music fading,
the wind calling through the waving *palmas*,
I bailing, Papito rowing
steadily across the watery darkness
to the shore I've made up on the other side.

—for Estel

VI

Estel

Your name, *Esther*, in your mother's shy *campesino* voice
sounded like *Estel*, though even then, unsure
whether I had misheard, I wrote it out,
and she nodded, yes, that looked like your name.
So that now at El Instituto Sordo Mudo
your white jumpers are all mislabeled
with the name you cannot hear, Estel,
learning to form those vowels in your mouth,
to read my lips explaining why you are here.
In the village, you were the errand girl,
carrying water up from the river; your head
cocked at an angle with the heavy loads
as if you were hearing, far off,
the sound of your new name being called.
La muda, the villagers shrugged when I asked

why you weren't in school, why you
were the little carrying horse, why you
didn't tell me your name along with the others,
flocking around me, begging for alms.
It was then I took an interest in you,
out there beyond the reach of the words I love.
Each time I came to the village, I lured you away
and wrote down words on the blank pages
I had meant to fill with poems after years
of my own silence; wrote down your name,
signed *you*, wrote *fishing boat, orange,*
whatever you pointed at I'd spell
until the paper darkened with your new words.
We walked the rocky coast looking for things
to name, I taking this opportunity
away from the watchful eyes of the villagers
to clean your cuts, feed you the oranges
you love, kill the lice in your hair
with a cream your mother couldn't afford to buy.
Once or twice I checked to see
if the words had taken, cutting the paper
in strips, pointing to something, asking you
to pick the name out from the pile in my skirt.
You seldom hit, the gulls were *waves*,
the palms were *fishing boats*, the seashells
tennis shoes, the world misunderstood—
but your name that wasn't really your name,
you always picked when I pointed to you!

Estel, at El Instituto Sordo Mudo,
they have fancier ways to teach you what I've tried,
but this is the gist of it: the world
expressed in words is yours, Estel.

You stand on the eight-year-old line, your pigtails
tied with white ribbons, dressed in white,
a blank intellience about to be filled
with your new life. But child of my silence,
listen, there will always be this sheerest gap
between the world and the word, *Estel*
for *Esther*, poems instead of the touch
I wish I could give you, now, so far
beyond my reach, deep in the mute heart.

DUTTON **PLUME**

THE LYRICAL WORKS OF JULIA ALVAREZ

☐ **IN THE TIME OF THE BUTTERFLIES.** They were the Mirabal sisters—symbols of defiant hope in a country shadowed by dictatorship and despair. They were the *Las Mariposas,* "The Butterflies," and in this extraordinary novel Patria, Minerva, Maria Teresa, and Dedé speak across the decades to tell their own stories—from tales of hair ribbons and secret crushes to gunrunning and prison torture. "An important book . . . emotionally wrenching . . . Alvarez has given us a gift of rare generosity and courage."—*San Diego Union-Tribune*   (274427—$11.95)

☐ **HOW THE GARCÍA GIRLS LOST THEIR ACCENTS.** Uprooted from their family home in the Dominican Republic, the García sisters—Carla, Sandra, Yolanda, and Sofía—arrive in New York City in 1960 to find a life far different from the genteel existence of maids, manicures, and extended family they left behind. What they have lost—and what they find—is revealed in the fifteen interconnected stories that comprise this exquisite novel. "Powerful, poignant."—*New York Times Book Review*   (268060—$11.95)

Prices slightly higher in Canada.

DUTTON

 PLUME

LITERARY FICTION

☐ **UNDER THE FEET OF JESUS by Helena María Viramontes.** This exquisitely sensitive novel has at its center Estrella, a girl about to cross over the perilous border to womanhood. What she knows of life comes from her mother, who has survived abandonment by her husband in a land where she is both an illegal alien and a farmworker. It captures the conflict of cultures, the bitterness of want, the sweetness of love, the power of pride, and the landscape of the human heart. (939490—$18.95)

☐ **WHEN THE RAINBOW GODDESS WEPT by Cecilia Manguerra Brainard.** Set against the backdrop of the Japanese invasion of the Philippines in 1941, this brilliant novel weaves myth and legend together with the suffering and tragedies of the Filipino people. It shows us the Philippines through an insider's eyes and brings to American audiences an unusual reading experience about a world that is utterly foreign and a child who is touchingly universal. (938214—$19.95)

☐ **THE UNFASTENED HEART by Lane von Herzen.** Anna de la Senda possesses an extraordinary empathy that draws to her a marvelous collection of lovelorn souls, who form a mischievous chorus and play matchmaker between Anna and a lonely widower. While Anna is rediscovering passion, her daughter Mariela in encountering it for the first time. Anna wishes to protect her from all worldy disappointments, but she cannot. "Evocative . . . a story of love and longing in a near-fantasy setting."—*Boston Globe* (272904—$10.95)

☐ **ENTERTAINING ANGELS by Marita van der Vyver.** Griet Swart's life is not exactly a fairy tale. Her once marvelous marriage has ended in divorce. She has lost her husband, her home, and her baby in yet another miscarriage. But late one night an angel appears on her doorstep and breaks her spell of sadness with a joyful sexual adventure. A modern-day fairy tale that is outrageously witty, unblushingly candid, and magically moving. "A real rarity . . . wry . . . hard to resist."—*New York Times Book Review* (273390—$10.95)

Prices slightly higher in Canada.